Create

Acquire

Protect

Preserve

The Wealth Secret

Create, Build and Protect your Future
the Penguin Way

The Wealth Secret

First published in 2015

Penguin Wealth
2 Raleigh Walk
Brigantine Place
Cardiff
CF10 4LN

02920 450143
info@penguinwealth.com
www.penguinwealth.com

Authored by Craig Palfrey, Chartered Wealth Manager at Penguin Wealth with contributions from Gavin Baos, Mike Carberry and Oliver Pughe of Penguin Wealth's Advice Team.

Cover design and editing by Oliver West

Foreword by Jeff Prestridge, personal finance editor of The Mail on Sunday

---

Foreword

For the past 25 years, I have made it my mission to explain the complex world of personal finance to newspaper audiences up and down the country. First, as personal finance editor of The Sunday Telegraph and now The Mail on Sunday.

I've tried to use money language that readers understand and words that encourage them to get on top of their finances. And whenever possible, I've emphasised the 'personal' in personal finance. After all, money matters do not have to be either boring or intimidating. Indeed they can be fun.

The quest to educate has been – and remains - a personal battle royal – and on occasion I've failed (sorry). But I will battle on regardless.

Sadly, it is a fact of life that the personal finance market is still riddled with bewildering terms, a complexity it shouldn't have, and a taxation system that even experts struggle to get their heads around.

Faced with these hurdles it is no surprise that many people fail to take financial control. Apathy rules.

Yet it should and must not be this way. With the State withdrawing its financial support for all but the most needy, and with more of us living well into our late 80 and early 90s it is vital we take care of our own finances more than ever.

That means we should be constructing our own personal finance defences: ensuring we have enough squirreled away for a rainy day or a financial emergency and that we have insurances in place to safeguard our household finances if long-term illness strikes or something happens to the family home.

This book provides a deep and rich mine of information on how you can build financial wealth. I love it because it adheres to all the principles I uphold as a personal finance editor. It makes a complex personal finance world seem less frightening and more welcoming.

Enjoy the read – and then put into practice some of what you have absorbed.

JEFF PRESTRIDGE, PERSONAL FINANCE EDITOR, THE MAIL ON SUNDAY

Contents

Introduction

The financial services market in 2015 is a very different market-place and industry from that of 2000 or 1980 or 1960. The change in operating standards, available financial products, the charges and costs of those products, regulation, the way advice is sought and provided, the technology, the information available, and the economic backdrop is considerable, arguably seismic - the ground has shifted so much!

However, despite this very different landscape and market, the **principles** that underpin good financial management and the acquisition of wealth have not changed at all. The basic structure of building and maintaining a successful financial plan for you as an individual, remain constant.

The basics are the same.

We will outline the basic structure, the principles and the 'rules' of sound financial management in the following pages. We aim to provide you with a crystal clear method to arrange your financial affairs so that whatever else happens you will develop wealth and thereafter protect this wealth.

The financial services market-place, in this respect, is irrelevant. But it's not just the market - the media, the adviser and sales communities complicate issues even further. The issues in the market are not your issues. Your requirement is to get from A to B and how you do this is based on a set of fundamental principles, which have not changed in the past 50 years and the reality is they probably have not changed since the dawn of time.

In the course of your journey along this financial pathway, you may use different structures to manage your money. For example 'wraps', one of the main money management tools used by investors today, did not exist 20 years ago. Fees, paperwork and tax considerations may be different and your expectation of future returns may have changed, but you will manage your position accordingly. However the basic principles by which you work towards creating and then preserving wealth remain constant.

But what does it mean to be wealthy or is being rich the ultimate conquest?

Rich is a wonderful word because it literally denotes more than just wealthy or possessing a lot of money. Yes, it can be *just* a scorecard. You can be rich by simply acquiring a great deal of money. The alternative definition is probably more appealing; it can mean bountiful and abundant.

This is the real definition of rich which we wish to pursue in these pages: a way of linking wealth to living; where money (or asset value) is merely a foundation for a better, *richer*, life. We cannot propose any fundamental methods of accumulating wealth unless it is broadened to how it relates to your life. In these pages we will show how using these principles not only provides for the acquisition of wealth but also how they can transform your life.

Follow these principles and everything else will lock firmly into place.

Principle No. 1

The lost art of saving

The one element of sound financial planning that has disappeared without trace is the **art of saving**.

In reality this is not an 'art' at all. It is a simple discipline – one that requires little creativity and no particular skill.

However it does require an approach and a dedication based on working around a simple starting point: saving should be *embedded* within any budget or cash flow financial plan. To work properly there should be no exception to this.

Most children are familiar with the idea of a piggy bank. Most will probably have one in their bedroom - with mum and dad popping odd coins and notes in every now and then. A pound here, a fiver there and then gifts from aunties and uncles at Christmas topping it all up. Little amounts put in regularly can produce a nice sum to pay for the special game or toy.

"Don't save what is left after spending; spend what is left after saving"

– Warren Buffet

A piggy bank and the concept of putting something aside established through childhood is the foundation for the savings principle that should be maintained throughout adulthood.

However, something has gone very wrong in recent decades as the savings habit has all but disappeared, sadly being replaced by the credit habit.

"Oh for the return of the life assurance salesman"

It may seem odd to you that, as professional financial planners, we are happy with the statement shown above!

Weren't all life assurance salesmen pushy and irritating people, selling expensive and inflexible products to the unwary and uninitiated? Wasn't the whole industry of commission-hungry sales forces just incentivised to shift products? Didn't they cause untold scandals and misery?

Well, the answer in most of these cases was actually "No!"

The reality was that in the main this nearly extinct industry of life assurance companies (e.g. Pearl, Prudential, and Allied Dunbar) achieved something quite magical, their sales teams 'forced' their individual customers to save. We use the word 'force' in a liberal way to describe the outcome which came from the selling activities of these sale people.

Over the past 20 years the number of life assurance representatives 'in the field' has fallen significantly, as has the UK savings ratio, see below (source: ONS NRJS).

UK Saving ratio

www.economicshelp.org | Source: ONS NRJS - nat income accounts Q3 2013

It may be that these two trends are coincidental. But we don't think so, we firmly believe that it is clear that the aggression of the Life Industry fostered a savings culture.

This has all but disappeared and now the emphasis is on 'DIY' saving. The motivation to save is with the saver, who no longer has the 'force' of a salesperson to encourage them. There is no evidence to suggest that the present generation has any discipline for DIY saving.

Here is an example of someone who benefitted from this now-extinct arrangement:

"I left school in 1972 and started work as an apprentice in a local factory. The money was poor but I was learning a trade and I moved through the various grades until I was fully qualified. By the age of 21 I already had five years of work experience and had started to earn OK money. I had few outgoings as I still lived at home, so I was actually able to do most of the things I wanted without too much trouble. It was around this time I met a guy who had been calling on my mum and dad for a few years. He worked for the Pearl. When he was in the house one day he asked if he could sit down with me for a while and discuss a life and savings plan."

"I didn't know anything about this sort of thing and didn't really want life assurance, but he showed me how I could save money into this plan and that over time it would build into a nice sum. I suppose I found it difficult to say no, so just signed up to £20 per month starting in 1977 for a 25 year term."

"I never really thought about it, it just seemed the right thing to do. As soon as I started paying it, I didn't miss the money at all and I got used to it going out. After a few years I left home and started my own family, the life assurance part of the plan was useful and as we started our own family we topped it up a few times, the monthly cost would increase a bit each time, so it eventually got up to around £50 per month as time went on."

"This just carried on through the years and although the Pearl guy left another one came along and in the 1990s I took out some more plans as I got better pay."

"Over time I had five different plans, never huge amounts but regular sums being paid out to cover my wife and kids should I die and savings to build for the future."

"It was 2002 when the first plan paid out. The cheque I received then was for a little over £14,000. Then the other plans started to pay out, £6,000, £11,000, £4,000 and another £11,000, the last one in 2010."

"I'm going to be 65 in a couple of years and I have a small pension built up through work and a private pension – from Pearl! This on its own is barely sufficient to keep me in the modest style I have become accustomed to, but with the state pension locking in, in a few years, it is all just about OK."

"The extra amounts from my savings, which are now around £60,000 in total, make all the difference, this is my safety net and my little luxury 'pot'. I can say for certain, two things about this: one is that I never saved a lot of money but I started saving a little bit every month and did so regularly throughout my working life and because of this I never really missed this money or felt short because of it; the second is that if the Pearl guy hadn't collared me all those years ago I don't think I would have ever got this going on my own. He was the reason I started. I don't know if the plans were good value or not but I know they made me a bit of money and I am happy because time has flown by and somehow despite never being that well paid I have managed to get in a position where I know I am OK."

This is a story, typical of millions of people who were "sold" policies by life assurance representatives. Maybe they did oversell at times and maybe some of the policies were not great, incurring heavy charges and inflexible terms. **But this is not the point.**

What happened here was that there was a happy meeting of interests. People who needed savings had savings and people who needed to earn a living, earned a living. As a result, a savings habit and culture was created.

This has all but disappeared and now people are asked to adopt their own personal savings habits. **But they don't.**

In addition, the lack of educational support is alarming; are our children shown the necessity, the power, or the value of saving? The current generation of savers is part of a generation that has been sold on credit and acquiring goods and services through borrowing.

It is also a generation of 'must have' and 'must have now'. The need for instant gratification and the materialistic demands of the current day somehow couple together to undermine the value of pursuing a longer term view.

In the past, the savings habit was passed down from one generation to the next, but the wild excesses of the past 20 years have all but destroyed this.

And yet, saving a little bit of every penny you earn is a central plank in any long-term successful financial plan.

One of the greatest books ever written about financial planning is 'The Richest Man in Babylon' by George Samuel Clason. It really is a classic and should be read by anyone serious about managing their money to create wealth for themselves. It stands the test of time and is written as a series of parables, beautifully simple in its propositions: there cannot be a better explanation of the value of saving.

It espouses the idea that wealth comes from saving one tenth of every penny you earn. This is the starting point and, in some ways, the end point too; do this and you *will* create wealth.

It also outlines how to deal with the money saved and the importance of managing the savings to ensure that wealth accumulates and this is how you become rich.

The lessons are countless and there are important points about discipline, frugality, enjoyment and pleasure. **It is a book which stresses that riches are more than the accumulation of money.** Please find it and read it – it is an inspiration.

We wish to expand upon the idea that wealth essentially comes from saving one tenth of all earnings. How is this achieved *regardless of the amount earned?*

We can translate this as follows:

In brief, the answer lies in a simple description of a teacher presenting his ideas to a group of workers. This group comprises high earners, low earners and those who sit somewhere in the middle. The workers bemoan their lack of spare money from their earnings.

The teacher asks how they spend their money. The answer is simple - they spend according to their earnings. The low income group spend a lot less than the high-income group. The spending adjusts according to the earnings, they do not all spend the same sums. How can that be possible?

How can they all spend 100% of their earnings when they earn different amounts?

This basic proposition stands the test of time; people spend proportionately. The conclusion therefore has to be that just about everyone can save 10% of income, because if spending is elastic, then there must be room for a 10% savings amount. Perhaps this 10% saving should be considered as another form of expenditure.

The 'norm' in 2015:

- Net Earnings £3,000 per month
- Spending £3,000 per month (or more!!)
- Saving £0 per month

What should be happening?

- Net Earnings £3,000 per month
- Saving £300 per month
- Spending £2,700 per month

Adjust the figures as you wish, the principle is simple, put the savings first – not last!

It really is a matter of discipline and expectation – if we were all disciplined to save 10% of our earnings, and this was an expectation the moment we first started to earn, then it would be achieved or achievable.

In later sections we will show how the power of regular saving starts to compound over time into large amounts.

We will also outline how saving can be aligned with your longer term goals. Visualising the future, and constructing a definitive link between the savings habit and your future self-interest and ambitions, will provide a real motivation towards saving.

Spending

One aspect of saving more is to spend *less*. In reviewing how you save you should balance this with a review of how you spend.

Many people claim that they have limited scope to save but close inspection of their spending habits would reveal the contrary. Limitation of unnecessary or inefficient spending can result in **savings**! Spending reviews are a recommended way of starting to think about how to save and how to save more.

Key factors of the First Principle:

- The modern financial world has become one built on credit; wealth creation comes from saving.
- The saving habit should be developed early.
- There are no longer sales people selling policies; individuals need to work with financial planners to arrange the required savings plans.

Saving 10% of every penny you earn is the foundation of wealth creation. Having a disciplined, regular, savings habit is the first principle of our financial plan. Now we will look at how you use the money you save to create a structured approach to managing it. Plus how important it is to manage everything with a clear goal and end game as a key point of your plan.

Principle No. 2
Your Goals

Develop your own personal 'business plan'

Creating and building a successful business requires developing a business plan which covers management roles, marketing and financial projections. This plan then acts as the basis for how the business is structured, managed and built.

Financial projections are used to create budgets and to act as a marker for how well the numbers are developing at various key points in time.

The business plan is likely to be the benchmark for how well the business is doing at different stages and will be updated and adjusted from time to time based on real experience as the business operates in its market.

It is strange that this basic principle of having a plan, using projections and developing budgets seems to be peculiar to the business world and the preserve of the business man or woman.

"People don't plan to fail, they fail to plan..."

Why are these same principles of planning, using projections and budgets generally ignored in the personal financial market?

Surely the basic structure of the business plan and its inherent value to act as a marker as the business progresses can be used for personal financial planning?

There is much to be said for people looking for a successful way to manage their finances to adopt this business approach and we encourage this. This is, in essence, our second underlying principle. However, we wish to apply a slight twist and our approach is to look at this personal financial plan (the equivalent of the business plan) as a map – a financial map.

Every individual looking to build wealth should have a financial map: one that is written down, has clear steps dictating how their money (assets, wealth etc.) will be managed and by whom, what their objectives are and how this all ties together.

There needs to be a strong element of working the map on a 'back to the future' basis; looking at where you want to be at various points in time. Working backwards from these points.

It is also important to be aware that each financial planning stage is different. Some people refer to these as 'life stages' – the concept that different actions/approaches need to be adopted during one's earlier years to the later years.

A single 20 year old, for example, setting out on their working life, will likely have a different approach to a couple in their middle years who have a family. They, in turn, will plan their finances in a way that would not work for a retired couple looking to spend their accumulated money in the later years.

The financial map, all future projections and scenarios will inevitably have to flow through these life stages – taking into account the variable nature and requirements of each stage.

How many stages are there? It is never **exactly** the same for two people, but in general, there are likely to be five or six distinct stages: early working years (beginning to earn; having disposable income for the first time), the starting-a-family years (getting married; buying a house; having children?), the bringing-up-family years (getting work promotions; schooling children, including through further education?), the empty nesting years (children leave home; couple or individuals find they are at their maximum earning power), early stage retirement (couple and individuals want to travel; continue being highly active), latter stage retirement (having comfort; looking to enjoy some peaceful time).

Of course this is a variable and highly generalised picture and maps could look very different for different people.

The realities of life: divorce, illness, financial misfortune are all examples of 'spanners in the works' which can throw the planning wildly off course – but these can be catered for.

Once created this map should be readily available and should be a constant reference point, reviewed at regular meetings and updated where necessary.

A real life example of how to create your map

David Evans is age 57 and is a director of Evans Materials, a business which he formed 20 years ago. He is married with two children. His wife, Mary, is a director of the business and his eldest child, a daughter Clare (age 28) also works within the business as a purchasing manager. His other child (Ben, age 25) is working elsewhere as a trainee surveyor.

David is a fitness fanatic, especially cycling which has become his passion in the past few years. He also plays golf. Both he and his wife like eating out, socialising, travelling and appreciate the nicer things in life!

His business has had a turbulent time over the past decade but is currently in an 'up' phase – this year profits are expected to be £80,000 on a turnover of £1.4 million; he is paid £49,000 salary, his wife £35,000; in a good year they may also receive around £40,000 in dividends (they own 76% of the company).

They both have pensions which are worth £160,000 (David) and £56,000 (Mary). They have contributions being added to this of £18,000 per year and £6,000 per year respectively.

Their company owes them £180,000 in loans they have made to it over the years.

They own their home – a detached four bedroom house with a current value of £600,000, they have a £350,000 mortgage (interest only) and other secured loans of £150,000. They have other borrowings amounting to approximately £30,000.

Their savings (bank, building society etc.) amount to £15,000. They have investments of £35,000 in stocks and shares ISAs.

	David	Mary
Assets		
Salary	£49,000.00 p/a	£35,000.00 p/a
Pension Fund Value	£160,000.00	£56,000.00
Pension Contributions	£18,000.00 p/a	£6,000.00 p/a
Dividends	£40,000.00 p/a	
Property	£600,000.00	
Savings	£15,000.00	
Stocks & Shares ISA	£35,000.00	
Loans to Company	£180,000.00	
Total Assets	**£1,194,000.00**	
Liabilities		
Mortgage	£350,000.00	
Other Secured Loans	£150,000.00	
Other Borrowings	£30,000.00	
Total Liabilities	**£530,000.00**	

p/a = per annum

Developing a map for David and Mary

All of the above describes their current position (in a summarised form) with some reference to their lifestyles and life requirements.

At the present time they have no defined plan of action, nor any form of constructed map.

What should they do?

Simple financial planning will assess their position and compare it with their future requirements. Decisions will then be taken accordingly.

Options to review are; enhancing savings, moving pensions to better-performing funds, switching their mortgage to better terms, rearranging their salary/dividend position for better tax results (i.e. to lower their annual tax bill) and so on. Any or all of which may be valuable and effective exercises to undertake.

However, we think this is **too** simple. This is short-term financial management which may well improve matters but does not create, enhance or protect their wealth in any meaningful or long-term, structured fashion.

Many people may baulk at this. A common objection to the idea of a longer term formula being applied is that "no-one knows the future".

Comments abound such as:

"But I don't know from year to year how my business is going to perform"

"I don't know how long I am going to live"

"I don't know what my health will be like"

"No-one knows what is going to happen to interest rates"

"No-one knows which party of government is going to be in power in 10 years or what the tax position will be or how much house prices will increase or decrease"

...and so on!

However valid each and every comment of this sort may be, it is no different to the vagaries and uncertainties of the business world. Yet all good businesses construct (and continually reconstruct) their business plans, projections, budgets and management approach.

The personal financial map is just the same, it takes on these uncertainties and unknowns and deals with them head on.

In which case, exactly what is the difference between a financial plan (of the traditional, simple type) and a financial map?

The answer is perhaps unexpected: the modern financial map is constructed around a cash flow analysis.

That is the difference.

Cash flow analyses are a way of looking into the future and predicting future expenditure (for decades ahead), then matching this expenditure with income. It is in creating this match between income and expenditure that will produce the financial planning requirement. As soon as the cash-flow analysis identifies anything untoward (especially periods of time where expenditure is not matched by income) a reason can be identified which allows for a reorganisation and informed financial decisions.

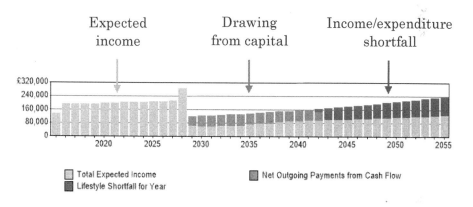

An example of how a Financial Forecast might look

"But I can't possibly know my expenditure in 20 years' time"

Really? Most people's expenditure requirements don't radically change over time and are actually predictable for very long periods ahead. Even where there are serious unknowns these can be dealt with by making assumptions.

At the moment Mr and Mrs Evans have expenditure which in its simplest form can be summarised as:

Monthly:	
Mortgage costs	*£1,500*
Insurances	*£300*
Credit Cards, loans etc.	*£400*
Household	*£200*
Shopping etc.	*£600*
Leisure	*£500*
Travel, holidays, car etc.	*£1,000*
TOTAL	**£4,500**

Their joint 'take home' income is currently around £5,500 ignoring any dividends they may receive from the company.

This year we know their expenditure and we know their income: they have around £12,000 they will accumulate in income over expenditure.

They have scope to deal with an interest rate rise and they can afford to live without the dividends they may be able to take from their company.

However, they expect the dividends to be £40,000 this year (around £24,000 after tax). This means that in year one of their cash-flow analysis we can show their expenditure and their income as follows:

Year One:

Total Net (after tax) Income	*£90,000*
Expenditure	*£54,000*
Surplus	*£36,000*

This means they have £36,000 to carry forward into year two - not a bad start...

We can do this year after year, populating our cash flow projection way into the future.

Of course, further down the line things may start to become more complicated because of the unknowns such as:

- What will happen to their business?
- Will it continue, will their daughter take it on?
- Will they sell it?
- If so, when and for how much?
- Consequently what will happen to their income and when?
- When will they retire?
- How will their expenditure change after they retire?
- What will happen if one of them dies earlier than expected?
- What happens if they need care or suffer ill health?
- What will happen with their interest only mortgage?
- Can the mortgage survive after age 65? (Some mortgages have to be cleared by then)

Ironically, the easiest thing to deal with is their expenditure. Mr and Mrs Evans enjoy life and don't see this changing even when they retire. They don't want to sell or leave the family home, at least not early on in retirement. They have a standard, normal, life expectancy.

In the main their basic expenditure, including their leisure and holiday/travel requirements, will stay the same (adjusted for their standard of living and inflation).This can then be placed into their cash flow for many years to come.

The requirement then becomes one where their income need has to be developed to meet this expenditure over time and allowing for variables.

If they retire next year it would cause a problem because there is no obvious income replacement for their current salaries; their pensions are not sufficient to do so and even if they received their dividends they would probably suffer a small shortfall.

They would still have the problem of their mortgage, which would ideally need to be cleared in eight years when Mr Evans reaches age 65. The cash flow analysis can include an assessment of an immediate retirement.

It will probably show future income/expenditure which do not match. It will highlight any glaring gaps (see the example earlier in this chapter).

Re-doing it to express a different pathway or map may show some clear timelines. For example, if they assume they will work for another three years and then hand the business to their daughter, they may be able to accumulate a further three years of £36,000 of surpluses each year (£108,000) and their pensions should hopefully accumulate through further contributions and extra growth.

Now the map may look very different: they could contemplate a major reduction in their mortgage.

However, even doing this shows that this stretches their requirement by placing an emphasis on the business which history tells them they cannot rely on. The business may be able to continue to pay dividends to them after they retire and they may be able to get their loan repaid, but they might not as their business is subject to ups and downs.

Their projected cash flow shows the dangers of relying on the business in this way.

Their map highlights two key financial planning requirements as they move towards and into retirement:

1. **They should try to ensure – if their business is simply handed to their daughter in a few years' time – that their future expenditure can be covered by their pensions.**

2. **They should aim to release the value of their shares (i.e. sell the shares) and organise for a repayment of their loan from the company to provide absolute security.**

Their map has produced a predicted/projected outcome which looks very favourable if they can achieve the second of the two options above. As a result they can start engaging in discussion with business advisers and their daughter about organising a progressive sale of their shares over the next few years and a repayment of their company loan.

The map provides a clarity to their thinking and planning, which includes a best case scenario (a sale of their shares etc.) and also a fall-back position both, of which ensure that their income matches expenditure over their retirements, however long they may live.

They test their plans and options against various scenarios trying to make sure, wherever possible that they are covered against as many outcomes as possible.

There are a number of reasons why the financial map works:

- Time is spent considering and focusing on the current and future positions. This produces a form of stress test and a concentration on making things work.

- There is an inherent, structural approach which turns the unknown into a set of possible future scenarios to help cover all possible outcomes.

- If you can plan for the worst and make sure you will be able to cope, the better-case scenarios will take care of themselves.

- The financial map is essentially a focus on your income and expenditure, making sure, as far as it is possible, that one will match the other as far into the future as you can see - not on financial products or chasing gains from investments without purpose. In this respect the dog is wagging its tail – so often in financial planning it seems it is the other way round!

- It creates a checkpoint which encourages regular reviews against the map as the journey progresses, allowing for constant adjustments and improvements to be made.

- It draws together all parties: husbands and wives, other family members, advisers, planners and other team members so that all relevant people are on the same page.

Working with their financial planner Mr and Mrs Evans were able to put together a plan to take them up to and into retirement. The plan covered many aspects including how to manage their business and the transition; how to maintain their lifestyle requirement and how to cater for their wider family needs.

Their plan was carefully calculated using future income/expenditure forecasts – providing them with clarity about timelines and how they need to allocate their money and assets moving forward.

They know that they have a clear pathway to pursue, but this could change (or have to *be changed*) over the years; which is why they will have regular six monthly reviews with their financial planner to monitor and judge the plan against the benchmarks set.

"Now the general who wins a battle makes many calculations in his temple ere the battle is fought. The general who loses a battle makes but few calculations beforehand. Thus do many calculations lead to victory, and few calculations to defeat: how much more no calculation at all! It is by attention to this point that I can foresee who is likely to win or lose."

- Sun Tzu on the Art of War

The map and your 'number'

In recent times there has been a host of material produced which aims to focus people on their 'number'. Put simply, the number is commonly defined as **the amount of money you will need for the rest of your life**. In some ways this is the same as the total expenditure defined by your lifetime map.

Your number, however, may also be different. It can be calculated as the lump sum value of your future expenditure. To explain this further, imagine this simplified example:

You calculate your expenditure for the next twenty years as being £20,000 per year, we will assume this is flat to keep the numbers simple. Level expenditure for many years is an unlikely prediction in practice, as expenditure needs will inevitably increase, even if this is just to cope with inflation.

20 x £20,000 = £400,000.
Therefore "your number" is **£400,000.** Or is it?

- Firstly, why 20 years? What happens if you live 10 years? Your number would be £200,000. Or 30 years? Your number would be £600,000?

- Secondly, is your number a straightforward calculation of the amount you need per year multiplied by the number of years left? Surely if you need £20,000 per year for 20 years, you don't need £400,000? Because if you had £400,000 now you would be able to make £20,000 per year last a lot longer than 20 years. Even if you only got 3% per year return on your £400,000, it would slow down the pace at which it disappears.

- For example, in year one you start with £400,000 and get 3% - giving you £12,000 'interest' or 'return' and you expend £20,000. So put simply, £400,000 + £12,000 - £20,000 = £392,000; so at the end of year one you have £392,000 not £380,000.

- Thirdly, if you need £20,000 per year maybe your number is £1,000,000 or £500,000? Because if you calculate that your interest return is going to be 2% per year if you have £1 million, you will be able to receive the interest each year knowing this covers your expenditure. However, if you can get 4% per year you need to have £500,000, if you apply the same thinking.

You can see from the examples above that your number can be anything from £200,000 to £1 million depending on the way you want to calculate it! Not particularly helpful if you are using 'the number' as a mechanism for efficient financial planning.

However, the number *is* valid. As with the cash-flow approach overall, if you aim to calculate your number, you will have the focus you need, ensuring that you have a financial plan in place to cope and make yourself comfortable.

The number, your number, will almost certainly be calculable based on a straight-line future expenditure analysis, mixed with a series of "what if?" scenarios. This will allow you to apply a number that you require at a certain point (e.g. on the day you retire) and make this *your number*. That figure will be **the accumulated lump sum** you need to be sure that **you will have enough money for the rest of your life** (however long that may be).

Is this precise? No. Is it reliable? No. However, it is going to be close enough (you cannot perfect the imperfect!). The exercise of assessing the figure and doing the calculations will be worth its weight in gold to you as it will help you link your future requirements to a structured plan; which is the key point.

This is one of the most important roles of a financial planner: helping you identify what sum of money you need to 'be enough'. If you can calculate the total sum and develop a financial plan to provide this sum, you will be sure to preserve your wealth.

Decumulation:

The Number is a concept which gives rise to a further idea and a new word for the Lexicon – the word being decumulation. This is basically the idea of spending your money as opposed to accumulating it.

The Number is the amount of money you need – once you have this you then need to work out how to spend it.

As with any part of the financial map – there will be major assumptions, various scenarios and means.

Most people are familiar with the idea that in accumulating wealth there are several important variables. For example how much you save and the investment return you achieve on the money you save.

If you save twice as much as your counterpart earning the same income and you get twice the investment return, you will accumulate far more wealth than they ever will.

Likewise decumulation requires careful appraisal of how you go about spending your money – and it becomes part of your plan.

Again, this is best illustrated by comparison. Imagine two people reaching 65 who both have £400,000 available to them for their retirement years.

One wants £20,000 per year to live, the other £40,000, taking into account their lifestyle and expenditure.

The way the money (the £400,000) is allocated and managed will vary – the 'decumulation plan' will need to be constructed in a completely different way. This may impact all sorts of aspects; what financial instruments to use, what investment return to target, what risk on any invested money can and should be taken; and so on.

One aspect of retirement expenditure requiring further comment is the mistake that many people (and their advisers?) planning expenditure often make when considering how monies will be spent in retirement.

The mistake is they assume rising expenditure in retirement. This is not a typical scenario!

Retirement expenditure typically rises then falls. If we consider a retirement period of 30 years for a married couple

– who retire around their mid-sixties, their likely pattern of expenditure is relatively high in the first part of retirement, sloping off during the second half. Most retirees will slow spending, all else being equal, during the latter stages of retirement.

Spending the money accumulated and working out how this is done is equally as important as working out how to accumulate the wealth in the first place!

Key Factors of the Second Principle:

- Creating a map provides you with a clear 'picture' of your future income and expenditure

- The main goal is to project your future expenditure as long term as you can

- Use cash flow financial forecasts to work out how to manage this future expenditure

- Work out your number as best you can

- Construct the plan in written form just as a business owner would write a business plan with financial forecasts

- Look at how you plan to 'decumulate'

Developing a financial map and projecting future cash flow, seeking to identify your "Number" is the second principle which will create wealth, as with any matter of this sort great 'planning' is arguably more important than great execution. Now we will look at one of the great pitfalls to avoid...

Principle No. 3
Avoid temptation and keep it simple

A good rule of thumb when it comes to managing your finances is this: assume that if anything looks too good to be true, it is.

Financial planning is inherently simple. Taking investments as the example, there is little more to investing than choosing the right asset areas in which to allocate your money. These asset areas should correspond to your financial map, risk approach and risk tolerance.

And there are essentially very few asset areas: cash, government bonds, corporate bonds, property, shares and commodities.

These can be split further, for example shares can be split into geographical regions (US, UK, Japan etc.) and/or into blue-chip (larger) companies or smaller companies.

Within these asset classes you have many ways of investing; for example you can invest directly or you can use funds. There are other alternatives and modern investing tools, such as derivatives.

"I can resist everything but **temptation**"

– Oscar Wilde

It is likely that your success as an investor will be determined by your asset selection. We examine this further in the next chapters and the conclusion is exciting. But before this we have to get as far away from the dangers of temptation as possible!

There may well be fortunes to be made from East African plantations or deep mining in Eastern Europe, but it is unlikely you will be making a fortune – especially if you have been offered the opportunity via a scheme or fund. The reason is simple: **if the investment opportunity was any good you wouldn't be getting the offer to invest!**

Whatever new or exotic fund or scheme you may see or may be put in front of you will only be for the benefit of the seller.

All the best deals in the market, whether for shares, property or other investment classes will be snapped up by insiders first and foremost: those in the know. It is very unlikely that anything which is truly a 'unique' or 'special' opportunity would ever see its way into a fund. There is also no such thing as 'a new way', if you ever read of a new trend or a method or system, be very cynical.

"I see great things in your past......"

In this day and age of super computers there will always be ways of tracking past investment results and trends to eke out a pattern of future movements in price. This can then be converted into a forward-looking projection, better still, a *predictor* of what is going to happen.

From there the investor can reap rich rewards. Sounds good? Well, the problem is there is not one bit of evidence - anywhere - that such approaches work. Indeed the evidence is compelling in the opposite direction; time and time again new systems appear, based on stock or asset selection from past trends and they *fall flat*.

For example, one of the leading UK newspapers published in 2014, as a front page money article, compelling 'evidence' that the US stock market tends to rise in the third year of a presidential term. By implication encouraging its readers to invest in US shares because (at the time of the article) we were getting close to the third year of the current US presidential term.

The 'evidence' is this: in three out of four of the presidential terms since 1900 the US stock market has risen in the third year and it is by some distance the best average return of any year with the presidential cycle.

This is backward looking nonsense! This sort of trend can be found time and time again if you look through the history books and correlations can be created with any number of non-related matters. The reality is that the US stock market tends to go up more often than it goes down and three out of four presidential third year increases is not too different from the average of all years.

Plus there is bound to be *one* of the four presidential years which is better than the others and there will be one that is the worst as well!

Finally, it doesn't take much to push something well above average. A couple of quirky years over time coinciding with third year presidential terms could easily make the statistics or average for *all* third years look good.

In scientific terms this evidence would be thrown aside as completely unreliable: the sample size is relatively small, the correlation almost totally non-existent, there is no discernible cause and effect here that investors can rely on. Indeed it could be argued that the fact that these third year returns have historically been better means it is likely the future returns will revert back to the average making it more likely that future third-year presidential terms will be poor!

The simple truth is this: there is no magical way of generating returns over and above the tried and tested. This simply means **pick the right asset mix for your circumstances**, find the best investment holdings within these asset areas and then manage this on an ongoing basis according to how events unravel.

Avoid anything that does not fit into this simple model.

Every single major scandal involves something 'clever'. Think Barlow Clowes, think Bernie Madoff, think Endowments or Split Capital Investment Trust Zeros. In every case the investment, scheme or product was in some way flawed - promising something which could not be delivered. High returns will almost always mean high risk whereas security will always mean low returns.

By always avoiding anything that looks too good to be true, or appears magical, you will avoid calamities. This will help you avoid unnecessary, or worse, unaffordable losses.

Temptation however is not restricted to unsuitable financial products or schemes or to the avoidance of clever methods.

Don't be confused by luck.

'The Black Swan' and 'Fooled by Randomness', written by Nassim Nicholas Taleb, are amongst the best books on investing. These are not without their detractors, but essentially they describe the very high element that luck and chance play in determining investment returns. Most importantly they are persuasive in explaining how success is often achieved by sheer good fortune.

Many commentators recognise the importance of luck – the simple fact that if you have enough players in the markets then by virtue of straightforward chance some will succeed.

The best way of thinking of this is to imagine 100 people walking into a casino each with £100. They are all tasked with playing roulette backing red or black and playing for an hour. They can back red or black on any spin of the wheel as they choose and bet any sum of money they like.

Typically, within one hour, there would be around 30 separate spins of the roulette wheel. On an average spin somewhere between 48 and 49 of the players will win, selecting the right colour.

Over the course of the 30 spins, or the hour, there will be a handful of players who will hit a lucky run, backing the right colour more often than not and getting their management of the money, the stakes they place on each spin, more right than wrong.

After an hour there should be some players who have turned their £100 stakes into £200 or maybe more, possibly much more. Most of the players will have lost money, some will have lost the lot. On the average, players will have less than £100 each.

Now parlay this situation into the markets; have the players who did well actually played better? It is true they may have managed their stakes better (working out an efficient way of maximising their return or minimising their risk) but otherwise they will simply have been luckier. Roulette is a game of chance and so it is with investment markets. It is entirely possible (in fact, probable) that with sufficient number of players (investors, fund managers, speculators et al) *some* will strike it lucky.

This is further enhanced by a phenomenon called survivorship bias whereby those who do well survive and those who do not disappear. This means that we tend to see those that have survived through this bias and don't see those that don't!

In this way, when we view markets historically the ones that have survived (probably including the luckier ones) become the focus and the ones that do very well, even spectacularly so, become the focus of articles and features, they write books and go on lecture tours. They become the influencers. Their views, methods and so called skills suggesting they have something magical for others to tap into and follow.

Anyone looking to master financial planning, to create and preserve wealth should be aware of how prevalent this phenomenon may actually be. In this respect past performance of a star investor or fund manager really is no guide to future returns. Simply because their luck may run out at any time.

Exuberance and the madness of crowds

Beyond luck there is a further danger lurking. History is littered with numerous examples of investment fads which have grabbed hold and taken millions of people (including some of the most initiated, informed and intelligent) along a pathway only to end in total, unmitigated disaster.

The fads lead to bubbles and bubbles burst.

This is born out time and time again. In recent times bubbles have appeared in technology share prices (in 1999/2000), Chinese stocks (in 2007) and in credit (leading to the financial crisis of 2008). Words such as exuberance, mania and delusion are common descriptions of the way these fads and bubbles appear.

The issue here for investors and wealth managers is to understand when something falls into such a category where it really is in bubble territory.

At the time of writing some commentators imply there is a bubble in gilt prices (i.e. the interest rate cycle is out of kilter and the cost of gilts has become ultra-expensive). Crowdfunding investments have become too popular and Bitcoin prices have gone out of control. Who knows? With any such thing it is normally only history which will inform whether these are fair assessments.

The important point for those of you seeking to create wealth is this: there are dangers in paying attention to anything which seems to be on a 'roll'. The behavioural aspect of all this is that people often feel they are missing out (a common element in the desire to own property) in comparison to others.

"My neighbour invested in X and made Y" or worse still "all my friends are buying this and making that and I'm not!" This is where fads starts, bubbles rise and madness sets in.

The dangers are real and ever present as the underlying emotional currency when it comes to money is generally fear and greed. Neither have any place in a well-structured approach to creating and acquiring wealth.

Keeping it simple

In business it is often said that there is little else that matters than buying something for £1 and selling it for £2, everything else is just a management function around this simple premise.

Of course that is probably too simple! However it is not a bad way to approach the subject of starting, building and expanding a business. If you can buy (or build) a product for £1 and sell if for £2 you will probably do very well.

It is the same with financial planning and wealth management. If you focus on saving a chunk of every penny you earn, investing well using an asset allocation approach and managing your risk you will find it difficult to go wrong. Step outside of this and the dangers start to appear.

Key Factors of the Third Principle:

- Keep it simple
- Avoid fads
- Don't be fooled or confused by luck
- If it looks too good to be true it probably is
- No-one has ever worked out how to consistently beat markets or shake a tree where money falls out
- Stick to basic and fundamental (and proven) investing methods

There is no need to do anything clever to create wealth, nor do you need to chase high returns from fancy schemes. Avoiding such temptations represents our third principle. Wealth will be created from pursuing a simple plan of regular saving and ensuring that the money saved is invested well. However, this will need to be done in a way that is risk efficient, which the next chapter consider in more detail.

Principle No. 4

Understand Risk

Understanding risk is a bit like trying to understand quantum mechanics, the more you study it, the crazier it becomes. Risk is one word but it has many different meanings depending often on the person considering it and their viewpoint.

The most commonly viewed position regarding risk is around the potential for loss on investments. In reality, this is just the tip of the 'risk iceberg'. However, it is a good place to start in trying to fathom a proper understanding of risk in all its meanings.

"In investing, what is comfortable is rarely profitable."

- Robert Arnott

It is probably safe to say that if a particular investment contained no risk, it would be very popular.

This is why the investment industry spends so much time trying to persuade investors and savers of the safety of any investment and why the word guarantee has played such a big part (historically) in promoting investments.

Supermarkets are famed for their skill in applying pricing and product placement in a way which entices maximum sales (and profitability) from their customer's whims and psychological fancies and so it is within the investment world.

"It's all in the mind"

Many investment companies apply as much (if not more!) attention and time to working out what sells and what makes people buy, or in this case invest, as they do to the actual investment process itself!

The marketing manager at an investment firm is often more important than the fund manager.

This is because the risk position is dominated by people's perceptions rather than the reality.

Investing, by its very nature, *has* to involve risk. The most common form of investing - buying company shares either directly or through a fund - has to be risky. This is for a simple reason: the price of the company's shares once bought are liable to fall and could even fall to zero and never recover. Shareholders therefore have to assume a risk when they buy shares.

At a simplistic level, a shareholder cannot risk more than their invested capital. There can be exceptions to this but they are exactly that – exceptions. The general rule of thumb, which is reliable, is that a shareholder invests *and risks* their invested capital but no more.

If you buy £10,000 worth of shares in Company X you may lose the lot, but you won't be asked to pay any more. The risk therefore in this example is that you invest and your whole investment could be gone tomorrow. The risk is **a total loss of money invested** and for many people this thought alone is enough to put them off investing.

This is why the marketing manager for an investment company will often spend so much time trying to downplay this risk and build in safeguards (however superficial this may be) to refocus the investor on the other side of the equation – the reward!

The start point, in our view, for dealing with all of this is to **understand** the risk being taken. Once the risk is properly understood it can be managed.

Staying with our example of investing into the shares of a company – the risk is total loss of money invested. Many people believe (with some accuracy) that this risk increases with smaller and newer companies and decreases with larger and older companies.

In other words, you are more likely to see a total wipe-out if you invest in a small start-up than if you invest into one of the top 30 or 100 companies (by size) in the UK.

However, if you care to look at a list of the top 30 or 100 UK companies 30 years ago you will notice it is a very different list to today's. This does not, of course, mean those companies no longer appearing in the top lists have gone bust (although some have) it just emphasises how companies' (of all sizes) fortunes fluctuate over time. **Even big companies go bust, although they are less likely to do so.**

Once we accept that investing into shares involves a total wipe-out risk, then there are two things we can do to mitigate and deal with it:

1. Spend a lot of time researching companies to try and find those with the best prospects and avoid those with the worst. Aim to get as much information as possible to flag the riskier prospects within the asset class of shares.

2. Reduce exposure by diversifying shares across many different companies, knowing that if every company we buy into has a one in ten chance of going bust in the next five years. If we buy into one company, we have a 10% chance of total loss; two a 1% chance and three a 0.1% (or 1 in 1000) chance. Once we buy the shares of ten companies (assuming the ratio of 1:10 chance of any company going bust on average) we have a miniscule risk of total loss.

It is in this second area that most investors will seek to reduce their risk and it is this that we are most interested in. This is an act of diversification and this is the way to reduce and manage risk.

Diversification in this case is simply the avoidance of putting all your eggs in one basket. We will study diversification in a slightly different context when we view our next principle in the following section.

However, for the time being we can establish that by spreading invested monies across a basket of shares we reduce the risk of total loss.

It is important to quantify this. All we are doing at this juncture is trying to manage risk to avoid 100% loss. There is no question that even with a very substantial spread of investment across many companies' shares the prospect of *a loss* still exists at a high level.

A short tangent at this stage is important, because there is a very striking factor in spreading the risk in this way that you need to understand. That is the optimum portfolio number.

If you want to create a share portfolio then you can select any different number of companies to hold in that portfolio. You could have a portfolio of one company or a portfolio of one hundred. How many companies do you think is the optimum size?

To explain the question a little further, at what point do you think you start to make little difference to the risk you are taking? In providing the answer we have to qualify a little:

- You hold equal value of shares in each company with your portfolio, so for example if your portfolio size is £50,000 and you select ten companies you invest £5,000 in each.

- The companies you invest into are non-correlated (so they are not all banks or oil companies for example).

If both options apply then the optimum portfolio size is between 12 and 18 depending on what piece of research you use/read. But it is always less than 20.

If you build a portfolio of 100 companies you have virtually the same risk as with 20 companies. The diversification factor tapers off almost entirely once you get above 20, and it makes no meaningful difference to how much risk you are taking.

By extension therefore, you do not need to over diversify. This is especially important if you are using funds as the bedrock of your investments and pensions.

Spreading your money across lots of funds in the same sector has virtually no impact on risk reduction. Due to their very nature and structure, funds are already diversified. Which sectors (or 'asset classes') you use and in what proportion will make a very big difference. However, when it comes to selecting funds - less is sometimes more!

This is what we mean by understanding risk. It is a measurable thing, where you can, if you study it, start to understand how you can work with risk quite easily.

Measuring risk

Many people are surprised that risk is, in some ways, measurable. It can be assessed, rather crudely, via volatility.

Volatility is the measure of risk based on the standard deviation of the return of an asset or a fund. The standard deviation in layman's terms is basically a figure which expresses how much the price of that asset or fund 'bounces around'.

Something which moves in small movements up or down (or up **and** down!) will have a low volatility because it has a small standard of deviation, something which moves around in leaps and bounds (in either direction) will have a high standard deviation and therefore higher volatility.

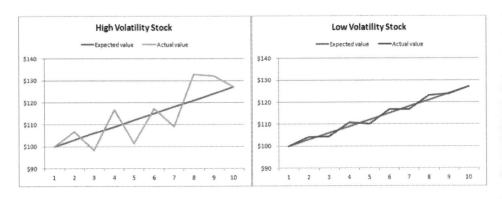

In some respects volatility is *a proxy* for risk rather than a measurement in its own right. However, for the purposes of looking at risk management and, most importantly, risk reduction, volatility is key.

The higher the volatility the higher the risk. However it is important to be cautious about a strict volatility = risk interpretation.

The problems with volatility as a measure of risk

Volatility is non-directional. It simply means how much something (a stock, bond, or portfolio) tends to move, regardless of the direction of the moves.

Risk, on the contrary, is usually understood as the possibility that something unfavourable happens. In investing it is the odds of your investment losing money.

One example – consider two shares:

Share A moves up 0-1% every third day, down 0-1% every third day, and more than 1% up or down every third day (this is not unlike many stocks in the real world).

Share B moves up 0-1% every other day, up 1-5% every third day, and up approximately 10% every sixth day.

Which share is more volatile? Share B because it moves 10% every sixth day.

Which share is more risky? In other words (as most people understand risk): which share has the greater prospect of loss? Share A. But Share B is more volatile, it can't lose money because it never goes down. Therefore, it is not risky at all.

Although a rather extreme (and seriously hypothetical example) it does evidence that using volatility as a strict measure of risk can be unreliable! In this respect volatility and risk are not the same thing.

When an asset (or fund or portfolio) is said to be volatile, it means that it tends to make big moves (up or down).

When an asset (or fund or portfolio) is said to be risky, it means that it can lose money (go down).

You don't lose money on assets that go up, even if they are volatile and the up move is really huge.

How volatility can underestimate actual risk

Volatility is normally measured as the standard deviation of returns. There are other ways, but standard deviation is by far the most common.

Nevertheless, there are some limitations. One of the most serious drawbacks is that volatility, when understood as standard deviation of returns (or something with a similar logic), does not adequately consider extreme events.

Public awareness of this idea is always greater following extreme events in the markets when many investors lose money on something that was estimated to occur once every X thousands of years but, in reality, happened to occur just during our lifetime.

The problem is that something with low volatility (it has low standard deviation of returns and its moves are *usually* very small), may once in a while makes an extremely big move (usually to the downside). This is, in fact, very risky but many investors are not aware of the risk because of the usual low volatility.

Typical examples of such securities are various credit instruments – highly rated corporate bonds or mortgage or credit derivatives which infamously started the big financial crisis of 2007-2008.

Volatility is only one measure of risk

If you want to measure risk without the risk of underestimating low-probability extreme outcomes, the only way to do it is by looking at maximum theoretical loss. This is a better method than looking at some expected value implied by a return distribution model that you have created based on historical observations. Although 0.01% probability of something looks like zero, it isn't. Although once every 10,000 years means unlikely, it could also mean tomorrow.

Of course, this does not mean that you should never invest in anything uncertain or anything volatile (because you wouldn't make any money). It means that while volatility is a useful measure of risk, it is not perfect and it should not be relied upon blindly.

Risk – how much can I lose?

The real question that most investors need to answer is 'how much?'

As described above, diversification can virtually eliminate the prospect of total loss, even relatively small amounts of diversification will achieve this.

However, the key question for most investors who decide (or need) to seek out the higher rewards offered by a higher risk portfolio is this: how much can I lose if I invest into X? If you know you won't lose the whole value, just **how far** could your money fall?

You will appreciate that this is not a question anyone can answer with precision or security. Strictly speaking the answer is 100% - you could lose everything, albeit the chances of this in a heavily diversified portfolio are so small they don't register except at the outer edges of possibilities.

If, in all reality, you will not be risking a 100% loss, what is the figure? Is it 99% or 70% or 50% or 30% or 1%? And does this figure really matter?

Yes, the figure matters. We will explore further on the concept of 'what goes down, doesn't go up by the same amount'. For example, a 50% loss requires a 100% recovery.

The further and faster the potential loss, the more danger there is that a recovery cannot be achieved.

It is impractical to consider *the extent of loss* (i.e. the real risk being taken) without considering timelines.

Someone investing over a time period of twenty years is going to have a different perspective on their risk than someone investing over five years. This is because, as we will examine shortly, the recovery time is important.

If you invest your savings and they lose 30% in the year after you have invested and you have an overall 20 year timeline and horizon, you have the propensity to recover this and more: your propensity for recovery is much less over five years. Therefore, all other things being equal, you can probably take more risk over longer investing time periods.

Risk against reward

Over and above your timeline you have to consider the risk in light of the potential reward. To illustrate this you do not want to have a potential for a 30% loss on an investment if it only has a prospect of a 3% per year return. If it has a good chance of a 10% per year return then you might consider the risk (the potential for loss) differently.

Ideally, you want to find the perfect risk/reward balance or certainly the optimum risk/reward.

There is a logic to this which we can all understand. Unfortunately there is also an inherent complexity because we are trying to create 'absolutes' out of things which are ultimately uncertain and defy scientific measurement. You can tell the temperature of a glass of water using a thermometer and, if the equipment is reliable, the measurement will be accurate.

However, no-one can tell you the *exact* risk you are taking or the *exact* reward you might get.

We have to accept this and work with inefficient measurements and use judgement, experience and assessments to produce the final answer.

This is done by reference to history and past performance and, although these are unreliable if you want precision, they are reliable enough to provide a framework.

We know, for example, that shares tend to produce a real (i.e. inflation adjusted) average annual return of around + 5%; property a return of + 4% and government bonds + 2%. We also know that shares are riskier than property, which is riskier than government bonds. A well-diversified portfolio of shares (or share based funds) will have a 30% downside at any given moment, property maybe a 20% downside, and bonds 10-15% and that the likelihood of such falls is also measurable based on past records.

Other asset classes can also be assessed on a past performance basis: all of this has unreliability attached and cannot be certain, however as stated it provides a framework, nothing more.

If we revert to our financial map, (to assess our targets and the rate of return we need or want to achieve), use asset allocation techniques (see the next section) and review and rebalance regularly, then we have something we can work with to help deal with the risks.

This just leaves one practical aspect of risk that we need to consider...

Your risk tolerance

All of the above concerning risk leads to a very stark conclusion – you will have a personal risk tolerance level **and it is this tolerance (which may change over time) which will underpin most of your decision making.**

In the past, until quite recently, risk position was generally dealt with by risk attitude. This was an assessment of the risk you were *prepared* to take. In financial planning terms, this meant you would be asked what sort of risk you wanted to take with your money, savings and investments and your financial plan would be created accordingly.

This was flawed for a number of reasons: one being that this gave too much credence to an overall behavioural approach and ignored the financial position.

One element of financial planning that an expert can bring to the party is to help an individual or a couple better understand how financial planning works, combined with some educational input on how to deal with risk. If the individual or couple are naturally risk adverse, maybe because of their upbringing or other early life experience, it could mean that they make decisions which are structurally poor.

On the other hand an 'I live for today' individual who has a care-free approach could be equally as poor in their decision making in the other direction.

Risk attitude asks too much of the individual to emotionally invest into the key decisions.

We know from the financial map what we want to happen, what we expect to happen and what we need to do to bridge the present and the future. The only question is can we tolerate the risk level required to pursue these plans? In this respect, the risk **attitude** of the individual is largely (if not wholly) irrelevant.

This is where these principles of managing wealth 'join up', because the financial map will show clearly what is required.

We saw this in action earlier, with the example of Mr and Mrs Evans and the construction of their financial map. The risks they were running were not obvious to them until their future, possible and various pathways were mapped out. The projected position at different times, depending on different scenarios, provided clarity about their risk tolerance, the extent of the risk and to – a significant extent – it quantified the risks for them.

They were able to see when their money would run out depending on different investment returns and income levels. They could judge how best to invest their available funds and allocate their assets to ensure their money would last for the rest of their lives.

This also allowed them to consider when to review their positions, offering them benchmarks to measure progress and act as a guide for future decisions. Having everything mapped out, with actual numbers attached (the 'quantification') was the key to their successful financial planning.

To highlight this further let us take the example of a 40 year old who is planning their finances from here through to their retirement and beyond. The predicted expenditure required into the future will show that by age 65 they need to have accumulated £650,000 (their 'number') to ensure they have the retirement to which they aspire.

This includes a requirement to save £4,000 per year, escalating these savings by 10% per year (i.e. in year two £4,400 is saved, year three £4,840 and so on) and the money growing in these savings by 7% per year. Their retirement pot (currently worth £78,000) has to grow by 7% per year.

If these requirements are shown this explicitly, this individual knows, with almost 100% certainty, they will not meet their objectives set down by the map if they invest into cash accounts. They will have to seek out higher growth from a portfolio of higher growth assets such as shares.

This comes with a risk as described earlier.

However, they have the advantage of a decent time period and can use asset allocation techniques accordingly.

Their risk tolerance is therefore positive, the individual can take the risk as they can tolerate the potential losses that could occur, either because they can overcome (over time) the losses or because their main 'downside' is not ruin – merely an adjustment to their map in the future and a downsizing of their future expenditure plans.

On the other hand a 57-year old planning to retire at 60 with £500,000 in savings and a pension has a very different position. If their map shows an income/expenditure which means they need £600,000 at age 60, then they will 'need' to achieve about 6% per year on their savings to reach this target over the following three years. They will also have to use real assets to achieve this target.

However, they no longer have the benefit of time on their side. The risk, for a fall of, say, 20% on their savings a few months after they placed the money in riskier asset areas *could not be tolerated*. Their risk tolerance in this respect is such they would have to take a defensive position in protecting their savings.

Risk tolerance is the key to determining what approach can or should be taken.

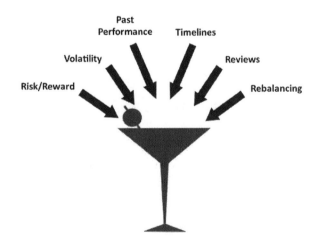

This chapter on risk has focused so far on investment risk; however risk comes in many forms. For anyone serious about financial planning there is another element of risk which must be factored in; the risk of things not going to plan *at all*. This is represented at its most extreme by the risk of death or the risk of serious and possibly critical ill health.

In many circumstances this is the starting point before any other matter is considered or tackled. Make sure you are protected. Nothing can devastate wealth or a family more than a death or a sudden serious illness.

"If I had my way, I would write the word "insure" upon the door of every cottage and upon the blotting book of every public man, because I am convinced, for sacrifices so small, families and estates can be protected against catastrophes which would otherwise smash them up forever. It is the duty to arrest the ghastly waste, not merely of human happiness, but national health and strength, which follows when, through the death of the breadwinner, the frail boat in which the family are embarked, founders and the women and children and the estates are left to struggle in the dark waters of a friendless world."

- Winston Churchill

This devastation extends to serious ill health and these threats (or risks) should be assessed as part of the financial map. The cost of protection is, as Winston Churchill stated, small in comparison to the benefit created. Of course, one hopes the insurance is never called upon, however there cannot be any meaningful financial plan put in place which does not have this as a central point.

Policies such as life assurance, critical illness insurance and ill health cover (such as protection against the loss of income, known as Permanent Health Insurance) are a mainstay, but putting these into place is just one step. Another consideration is whether these or other investments should be placed under a trust.

There is little in the financial world that is more misunderstood than trusts and their usages.

The common misconception is that trusts are complex, expensive and only for the very wealthiest. These are, indeed, misconceptions. If you would like to learn more about Trusts and how they could help you visit www.penguintaxplanning.co.uk.

The use of trusts is a bedrock of getting plans in place which have a clear direction attached to them. Many consider trusts to be a tax planning device; putting assets or benefits out of the reach of the taxman. They can and often do have this feature. However trusts are as much about a written direction as much as anything else.

A trust allows the individual to write down what they intend to happen and where benefits should go; they can be used to avoid assets being claimed by the divorcing spouse of a child or grandchild; against bankruptcy; against business assets ending up in the hands of a fellow shareholders' family by default and so on.

A trust can be applied to a pension plan so that the value of the pension goes straight to where you want it to go.

In the life assurance example, a trust can ensure that in the very unfortunate event that your life policy pays out, the life assurance does not become part of your taxable estate for Inheritance tax purposes.

They can also ensure monies are paid out immediately, whereas otherwise they might be delayed for years.

Trusts are, in the main, easy to put in place, uncomplicated and crucially, they are legally robust, which means that their use (and effectiveness) is not open to challenge.

Key Factors of the Fourth Principle:

- Risk is inherently part of investing
- Focus on risk management rather than the reward
- Try and understand and wherever possible measure the risks being taken
- Remember it is your risk tolerance that is most important
- Diversification is a proven way to control and reduce risk
- Insurance is a central plank in protecting wealth
- Trusts should be used to manage certain non-financial risks, such as death, divorce and bankruptcy

Dealing with risk requires a 'cocktail' approach; you have to throw a lot into the mix to understand risk, deal with it and have a practical approach to it. There is no point in creating wealth if you then take risks which ruin it. You cannot bet 'red' or 'black' with your money you need to diversify and then quantify as much as you can, keeping a close eye on matters continuously and adjusting as you go. However, if there is one key ingredient in this cocktail it is getting your diversification as right as you can, which is where we will turn to now...

Principle No. 5
Get your asset allocation right

The main aspect here is a simple proposition which follows on from our previous section on risk:

Diversification in uncorrelated assets leads to a reduced risk without diminishing the expected returns!

This is so important it is worth repeating: if you get your asset allocation correct you can reduce your risk, without reducing your potential return.

What is meant by asset allocation?

Asset allocation involves dividing an investment portfolio among different asset categories, such as company shares, bonds, property and cash.

The process of determining which mix of assets to hold in your portfolio will be based on a number of factors, determined by your time horizon, your risk tolerance and your financial targets (established by your financial map).

The asset allocation mix is liable to change over time as you get older.

"How many millionaires do you know who have become wealthy by investing in savings accounts? I rest my case."

- Robert G. Allen

Why asset allocation is important

Including asset categories with investment returns that move up and down **under different market conditions** within a portfolio can protect against significant losses.

Historically, the returns of the major asset categories have not moved up and down at the same time. Market conditions that cause one asset category to do well often cause another asset category to have average or poor returns. This is mostly, but not always, the case.

By investing in more than one asset category, you will reduce the risk that you will lose money and your portfolio's overall investment returns will have a smoother ride. If one asset category's investment return falls, you'll be in a position to counteract your losses with better investment returns in another asset category.

Asset allocation is important because it greatly impacts on successfully achieving your financial objectives.

If you don't include enough risk in your portfolio, your investments may not earn a sufficient return to meet your targets. On the other hand, if you include too much risk in your portfolio, the money for your goal may not be available when you need it.

A portfolio heavily weighted in shares or share-based funds, for instance, would be inappropriate for a short-term goal: such as saving for a deposit on a house, a holiday or new car.

Determining an appropriate asset allocation model for a financial goal is a complicated task. Basically, you are trying to pick a mix of assets that has the highest probability of achieving your goal at a level of risk you can accept. As you get closer to meeting your goal, you'll need to be able to adjust the mix of assets.

The connection between asset allocation and diversification

Diversification is a strategy that can be summed up by the timeless adage: "Don't put all your eggs in one basket." The strategy involves spreading your money among various investments in the hope that if one investment loses money, the other investments will more than make up the loss.

Many investors use asset allocation as a way of diversifying their investments among different asset types. Other investors deliberately do not. Consider two cases: a twenty-five year-old saving for retirement may invest entirely in shares; a family saving for the down payment on a house may invest solely in cash equivalents. Both these scenarios may, under certain circumstances, be reasonable examples of asset allocation but neither strategy attempts to reduce risk by holding different types of asset categories. Choosing an asset allocation model won't necessarily diversify your portfolio. It is diversification which creates the risk reduction.

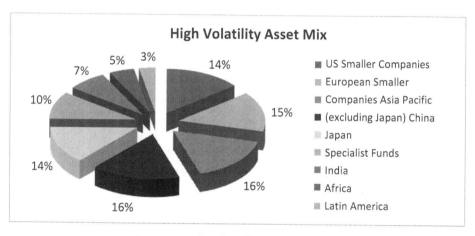

An example of a diversified portfolio

Diversification

A diversified portfolio should be diversified at two levels: *between* asset categories and *within* asset categories. So in addition to allocating your investments among shares, bonds, cash and other asset categories (for example property and commodities), you'll also need to spread your investments within each asset category. The key is to identify investments in segments of each asset category that may perform differently under different market conditions.

One way of diversifying your investments within an asset category is to identify and invest in a wide range of companies and industry sectors. But the share portion of your investment portfolio won't necessarily be diversified if you invest in only four or five individual stocks. You'll need at least a dozen carefully selected individual stocks to be truly diversified.

A second way of diversifying is to make use of funds. Achieving diversification can be challenging so many investors find it easier to diversify within each asset category through the ownership of funds rather than through individual investments or holdings. A fund is a company, or trust, that pools money from many investors and invests the money in stocks, bonds, and other financial instruments. Funds make it easy for investors to own a small portion of many investments. A share based index fund (a 'tracker'), for example, owns stock in potentially hundreds of companies.

Be aware that a fund investment doesn't necessarily provide instant diversification, especially if the fund focuses on only one particular industry sector, such as technology shares. If you invest in narrowly focused funds, you may need to invest in more than one fund to get the diversification you seek.

Within asset categories, this may mean considering large company funds as well as some small company and international funds for instance. Between asset categories, this may mean considering share funds, bond funds, and money market funds.

Changing your asset allocation

The most common reasons for changing your asset allocation are a change in your time horizon or a change in your circumstances. As you near your investment goal, you'll likely need to change your asset allocation.

For example, most people investing for retirement hold less risky assets (such as shares) as they approach retirement age.

You may also need to change your asset allocation if there is a change in your risk tolerance, financial situation, or the financial goal itself.

A disciplined investor will not change their asset allocation based on the relative performance of asset categories, for example, increasing the proportion of shares in one's portfolio when the stock market is hot. Instead, that's when they "rebalance" their portfolios and in effect do the exact opposite. Remember the key is too buy low, sell high!

Rebalancing

Rebalancing is bringing your portfolio back to your original asset allocation mix. This is necessary because over time some of your investments may become out of alignment with your investment goals.

You will find that some of your investments will grow faster than others. Rebalancing will ensure that your portfolio does not overemphasize one or more asset categories, and you'll return your portfolio to a comfortable level of risk.

For example, having determined that shares should represent 50% of your portfolio, you find that after two years they have increased in value and now represent 65% of your portfolio. You will need to either sell some of your shares or purchase investments such as bonds, from an under-weighted asset category, in order to re-establish your original asset allocation mix.

Portfolio example

Asset category	Starting allocation	Allocation after two years
Shares	50%	65%
Bonds	25%	18%
Property	15%	8%
Commodities	5%	7%
Cash	5%	2%

Some asset categories have gone up, and some have gone down

You would sell some of the shares and commodities and buy bonds, property and cash to return to your starting portfolio percentages.

Over time, this should encourage buying things as they get cheaper and selling things as they get more expensive.

When you rebalance, you will also need to review the investments *within* each asset allocation category. If any investments are out of alignment with your investment goals you will need to amend them to bring them back to their original allocation within that asset category.

There are basically three different ways through which you can rebalance your portfolio:

1. Sell off investments from over-weighted asset categories and use the proceeds to purchase investments for under-weighted asset categories.

2. Purchase new investments for under-weighted asset categories.

3. If making continuous contributions to the portfolio, increase the contributions to under-weighted asset categories until your portfolio is balanced again.

Before rebalancing your portfolio, you should consider whether any changes you decide to make will trigger transaction fees or tax consequences. Your financial planner can help you identify ways to minimise these potential costs.

Moving money away from an asset category when it is doing well to an asset category doing poorly may not be easy, but it can be a wise move. By cutting back on the current 'winners' and adding more of the current 'losers'; rebalancing has the effect of buying high and selling low - Usually a pretty good way to make money!

When to consider rebalancing

You can rebalance your portfolio based either on the calendar or on your investments. Many financial experts recommend that investors rebalance their portfolios on a regular time interval, such as every six or twelve months.

Others recommend rebalancing only when the relative weight of an asset class increases or decreases more than the certain percentage that you have identified in advance. The advantage of this method is that your investments tell you when to rebalance.

How to determine your asset allocation in the first place

Once it is understood how important the asset allocation process is and how getting this right can make such a difference, a stark question looms into view: how do you decide which asset allocation to pursue?

The problem with financial planning is the uncertain and unknown future position of so many critical factors. Therefore, we have to rely on historic patterns and cycles. For example, over time shares have outperformed gilts and gilts have outperformed cash.

We can therefore only apply assumptions to future returns (which can be adjusted through cycles and will normally be applied as a real return i.e. the return above inflation) and we know the level of risk – again based on historic performance.

Using these assumptions, portfolios can be constructed which aim to meet the time horizon objectives. The objectives will be set out within the financial map previously constructed. From this, a suitable asset allocation can be put together for any given portfolio.

A typical example for a 40 year old with a pension plan targeted to age 60 could look like this:

- Shares - 60%
- Gilts - 20%
- Property - 10%
- Commodities - 10%

This asset allocation mix can be reviewed regularly to see how it is working in line with the objectives set within the financial map. It can also be rebalanced in accordance with the shifting mix that occurs as a result of performance and any possible divergence in performance that may have occurred.

These review and rebalance exercises are crucial to longer term success.

How to choose the underlying investment structure and the vehicles to use

The asset areas can be split further within the asset class, so the shares element (which is 60% of the total) may be as follows:

- 15% UK Larger/Blue Chip Companies
- 15% UK Smaller Companies
- 10% US Companies
- 10% European Companies
- 5% Asian Companies
- 5% Emerging Markets.

The Gilts (total 20%) may be:

- 10% UK Gilts
- 10% **Overseas Bonds** (bonds being the overseas equivalents of gilts).

As previously described the spread is not that important to your risk reduction especially if you use funds. If you do not use funds, you only need to use 15 individual holdings (provided they are not correlated) in any particular asset class to optimise your risk reduction.

Whatever structure you use, direct (buying shares, gilts, bonds individually) or indirect (using funds) there will always be an emphasis on finding quality. This may be stating the obvious, however, there is a large amount of choice and many options do not have that quality.

What do we mean by quality?

- A proven track record
- Consistency
- Good management

In many respects these three quality tests will cover any investment, direct or indirect.

There is a regulatory warning that past performance is no guarantee of future returns, which often gets misinterpreted. The implication is that you should ignore past performance - this is not what this warning is about. Past performance is an important but unreliable indicator. If something has performed at 8% per year for the past five years you should not expect, or rely upon, it to do so for the next five. However, if the performance has consistently been better than its peers, or similar investments/types, it is a factor worth considering.

In addition past performance *on its own* is just one aspect. Other considerations include:

- How has this performance been achieved?

- Has the investment been overly volatile? If yes and volatility is higher than normal for this type of investment it would imply higher risks have been taken and the return may be the result of unreasonable risk or luck has played a part.

- How consistent has the investment been?

- Are there any other factors in play? For example, has there been a management or structural change to the investment?

Direct or indirect holdings?

Once you have decided on your asset allocation you may then need to decide how to hold those assets. If your asset allocation dictates 15% of your wealth should be in UK shares, do you hold them in a basket of shares you select or do you hand them to a fund manager who runs a UK Equity Fund?

In most cases investors will choose the latter, but this is clearly a decision that can be taken with your financial planner based on your tax position; how confident you are to take this on yourself; whether you want to invest actively or passively (see below) amongst many other factors.

In reality, sometimes you just have to buy a fund. For example, if your asset allocation determines you should have 5% of your money in Emerging Markets shares you should buy these yourself. Try ringing up a stockbroker in Indonesia for example!

Funds are generally the route forward for most investors. They offer the chance for the investment to be handled by an expert, for diversification to be created by the fund structure and then crucially, in some cases, for currency risks to be managed.

'Vehicles'

In addition you will have to determine the vehicles you use to hold your money. A vehicle is a type of account, for example; an ISA or pension, a Unit Trust, an OEIC or an Investment Trust. Should you use VCTs or EISs? All of these different investment types may have tax implications, different advantages and disadvantages, costs and other implications.

Active or passive?

The final additional requirement is to determine whether to invest actively or passively. The former uses investments or funds that have an active approach where the fund manager, or whoever else looks after the investment, makes decisions such as what to hold in the fund and when to buy and sell.

Investing passively follows the market index. The fund manager will simply allocate the holdings to a basket of shares which mirror the average of that market.

You will see therefore that there is a process here that needs to be applied. This is a way of ensuring that you get the right asset allocation, and that the eventual make-up of your portfolio or holdings is exactly tuned to your situation; your risk position, your tax position and in line with your long term goals.

It is getting this combined approach in place which ensures that your 'holdings' are matching the requirements of your financial map.

Key Factors of the Fifth Principle:

- Getting your asset allocation right is more important than timing or what funds you might use; it is the most important part of the investment process
- Match your asset allocation to your risk profile

- Then select the best funds or underlying holdings

- Use rebalancing as a central part of managing your asset allocation longer term

---

Asset allocation is the process which determines how your investments perform, which has a direct impact on how your wealth accumulates and how well you protect it. Your eventual success, and the extent of this success, will be a factor of your asset allocation decisions. Managing your asset allocation involves regular rebalancing to keep everything on track. Getting your asset allocation right is a key principle in managing your wealth. Understanding some mathematical anomalies will help cement this as we shall examine in the next chapter.

Principle No. 6

The unbelievable power of some basic mathematic principles

Apparently we are just a few years away from driver-less cars. The future, it appears, will be roads full of cars with passengers only.

These cars will be driven by computers. They will be safer, more efficient, and more comfortable and will get you from A to B more quickly. Computers and modern technology can do so many things better than we can as humans.

Let us return to money. What would happen if the human element was taken out of money management, saving and investing?

It would probably all be done much better!

"Two plus two equals four, most of the time"

As discussed in earlier chapters it is human intervention which often causes problems. Temptation, acting emotionally, irrational fears, greed and misunderstood risks are all factors of poor money management.

One of the great aspects of cash flow financial modelling (your map which we covered earlier) is that it aims to provide a mathematical, structured, and disciplined base for good long-term financial planning.

Let us take this one step further and look at a couple of simple structural approaches to investing which are based on core mathematical principles.

The first is compounding. Even Einstein is reported to have stated he couldn't really understand compounding but he knew its power!

The simple way to look at this is to imagine you have £1,000 and you *must* invest this for 20 years and whatever you obtain as a return is what you get back in 20-years' time.

Let's look at the different eventual return you might achieve using five possible annual average returns: 2%, 4%, 8%, 12% and 16%.

Now before looking at the results, ask yourself what you expect the final differences to be – have a guess first. Bear in mind that 16% is eight times the return of 2% - so are you expecting eight times the pot size after twenty years? No because you know that compounding will increase it more than eightfold; so what do you expect?

Here are the results for £1000 invested:

% per year	Average return after 20 years
2	£1,486
4	£2,191
8	£4,661
12	£9,646
16	£19,460

Take any starting figure you feel is right and multiply it. For example, two people starting with £100,000 – one gets 4%, the other 12% - the difference is nearly £750,000! Look at the £1,000 example on a graph and you can see what is known as the stretching effect taking place:

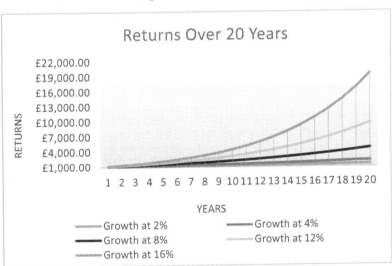

This demonstrates the compounding benefit which widens over time. The above example shows the stretch over 20 years but if you really want to see the power of stretching look at what happens if you project further 40 years.

Again, for £1,000 invested:

% Per year	Average return
2	£2,208
4	£4,801
8	£21,724
12	£93,051
16	£378,721

Again let's show this on a graph:

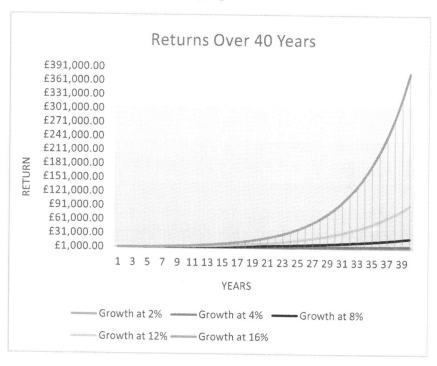

You might think this is a bit extreme, 40 years is a long time. It is however, the timeframe for anyone starting a pension early in their career.

The graph also shows how much *less* they have to save if they get a reasonable return. For a retirement fund of £378,000 at 65, someone needs to save only £1,000 at the start of their journey and make sure they get 16% per year thereafter to achieve their target. Easier said than done! Someone who wants a retirement fund of £378,000 and gets 2% per year return will have to save hundreds of thousands from their earnings. The contrast is stark! But didn't we say in chapter one that we should save 10% of everything we earn anyway? Yes, we did. Achieving real wealth, real financial success requires a combination of these two elements: regular savings discipline **with** great compounded returns. Do this and you will create and build serious wealth even with low starting amounts.

To consider a second example we start with another graph which compares the actual returns achieved from the UK stock market since 1970 when dividends are reinvested:

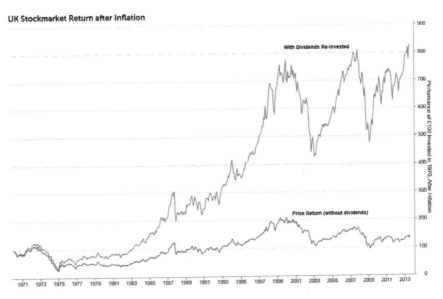

UK Stockmarket Return after Inflation

Source: Macrobond, MSCI UK Net Total Return and Price Return Indices

Using shares to build wealth is largely ineffective if you buy shares, hold them, receive dividends and then spend the dividends. However, if you invest in shares, hold them and reinvest the dividends you receive back, into further shares, **you create wealth.**

Another financial quirk is the 'recovery of losses phenomenon'

Imagine you invest £50,000 in a fund or a share and it falls by half (50% drop) over two years, the value of your investment will drop to £25,000.

The investment then *increases* by 50% in the third year. So it has fallen by 50% and then risen by 50%. The value after three years is £37,500.....It is still £12,500 lower.

This is because a 50% fall has to subsequently recover and rise from that point *by 100%* to return to the start point.

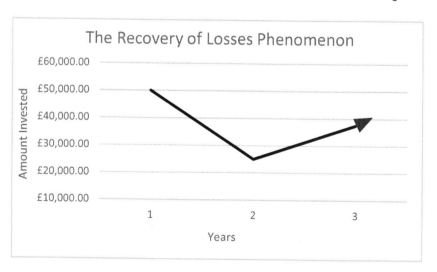

This is evidence of how destructive losses can be.

Here are some of the subsequent increases you would need following a loss, with some tiny approximations:

% Loss	% Recovery needed for a return to your starting point
10	11
34	50
50	100
80	400

The trend here is obvious, the greater the fall the greater the subsequent recovery required. Losing 10% of value only needs an approximate recovery of the same value in the other direction, a loss of 80% requires an astonishing return, which is unlikely to occur.

A quick story to illustrate this in a real life way:

In 1999 Tariq, was a 27-year old software engineer in London, earned a sufficient enough wage to allow him to accumulate savings of around £16,000. He watched with interest as the boom in technology started to take hold and looked at the money being made by investors in 'tech' stocks and funds.

Friends and colleagues told him stories of buying shares for £3,000 and finding that within a few months they had doubled (or more) their money. One friend, using borrowed money, was making over £2,000 per month in profits.

Later that year Tariq decided that he should get involved and bought into some technology funds as well as some direct technology company shareholdings.

He committed half his savings (£8,000) and within four months his portfolio had increased to £13,000. This return of around 60% in just a few months encouraged him to invest his remaining savings in early 2000 and within a month his portfolio was worth £24,000.

Then, suddenly, bang! The technology boom became a bust and the value of technology investments started to fall and fall quickly. Tariq didn't know what to do for the best. In just a few weeks his £24,000 was worth £18,000, a few weeks later £15,000 and within a year £6,000. On several occasions he considered cutting and running but every time he decided to do so the value just kept on going down. He tried to hang on and wait for a recovery or at least a temporary halt in the slide.

The halt eventually came when his portfolio bottomed at £4,900, a fall of around 70% on his original starting sum. Thirteen years later his portfolio is now worth £12,700. This is an increase of 160% from its lowest point and not a bad return over the last thirteen years. However he is still down 20% over the 15 year period.

It is not just the financial loss he has suffered, it is also the 'opportunity cost': the cost compared to what he could have done with the money he had available to him in 1999.

The extent of his investment loss is too steep to ever reasonably expect any recovery.

This is especially pronounced for people who are approaching or are in the early years of their retirement.

Take Mr and Mrs Evans, who we encountered earlier, in chapter two. They were keen to examine how and when they could retire given their existing make up, future scenarios and lifestyle requirements.

They experienced a cash flow forecast approach which assessed the impact of different outcomes at different times. This will have included illustrating the impact of heavy losses on their invested/saved money. In their situation and with their needs, they would be in no position to cope with a heavy downturn in values; given how they need this money to help with income and expenditure in retirement.

This would, in turn, therefore help them to decide on the correct investment strategy through the years ahead, because they would see how difficult it can be – and critically how long it can take - to recover heavy losses.

Mathematical principles applied to practical day to day questions and considerations

It would be incorrect to consider this section merely as a discourse on some simple mathematics. There are very real mathematical calculations that need to be applied to everyday financial decisions faced by investors and savers.

The one we wish to examine is also one of the most emotive: should you use a capital sum to pay off a mortgage?

Imagine you are in the following position:

You are aged 55, in a steady employment, earning sufficient money to comfortably afford your lifestyle and accumulate savings for your retirement. You have an interest only mortgage of £200,000, due for repayment in 12 years' time.

Your elderly aunt dies and leaves you £200,000. Do you use the £200,000 windfall to clear your mortgage?

Most people when faced with this question would answer either yes or no. However, this may be the wrong answer! The best answer should be – "it depends....."

Firstly, there is evidence that many people would like to pay off their mortgage for behavioural or psychological reasons regardless of any mathematical considerations. It may make them feel better, sleep more soundly at night and generally improve their mood!

On the strict financial front the answer is more complex. Many factors need to be considered before a decision can be reached, these include (and this list is not exhaustive):

- What is the cost of the mortgage (i.e. the interest rate?)

- What are the prospects for these costs increasing (or decreasing?)

- How easy would it be to get another mortgage in later years?

- What return could be achieved by investing the capital?

- What is the risk on the invested capital?

- How does the repayment of the mortgage fit into your financial map, today, in 5 years or in 12 years?

- If you repay the mortgage *now*, saving the monthly repayments, what could you do with that monthly sum? Would you use it to boost your pension? Would the tax relief on contributions generate a higher sum than investing the capital between now and your retirement, or your anticipated mortgage repayment date in 12 years' time?

- What is your tax position, especially with respect to inheritance tax? Can you leave the mortgage in place as a liability against your estate and invest the inherited capital to move outside of your estate? This could have the effect, at current tax rates, of saving £80,000+ in future tax liability for your beneficiaries.

Clearly many of these factors and questions are intertwined. The question "should the mortgage be paid off?" requires a careful analysis and appraisal of all these factors. It is then, and only then, that an answer can be reached.

By reverting to the power of your financial map and preparing a cash flow analysis you can compare different scenarios to discover and understand their impact.

You could for example run the following scenarios:

1. Pay off your mortgage now

2. Pay off your mortgage in 12 years

3. Pay off your mortgage at some other time in between

4. Change the assumptions to investigate happens if you invest the money instead at different rates of return and/or mortgage costs change and so on...

Preserving your money from unwanted taxation

We examined the power of compounding earlier in this chapter. The pursuit of an efficient tax strategy within your financial planning is directly linked to this.

In exploring this further we wish to make it clear that we are assuming you have no political or other view which suggests you want to pay more rather than less tax. The value of paying less tax is obvious, the money you save can be used to build your wealth amount. As we know extra amounts accumulate very nicely.

If you look at two investors who pursue the exact same strategy for 30 years, both getting a 5% per year return after charges, but one pays tax of 20% on the return whilst the other gets it tax free – **the tax payer will have 46% less in savings at the end**.

Seeking out tax efficiency (as opposed to tax inefficiency) can create greater returns regardless of any other factor.

Another area that highlights this and is a further quirk of the tax system, is in regard to inheritance tax where there are high tax allowances versus a static rate.

The table below shows the effect of taxation on different estate values assuming an inheritance tax nil rate allowance of £650,000 and a 40% flat rate of tax.

Estate Value (£)	Tax Payable (£)	Rate of Tax as % of the Estate
£200,000	0	0
£600,000	0	0
£1,000,000	£140,000	14%
£2,000,000	£540,000	27%
£4,000,000	£1,340,000	33.5%
£6,000,000	£2,140,000	35.67%

Governments are clever because they know the power of freezing an allowance. Imagine today you have an estate of £1,000,000, your house, savings and worldly goods add up to £1m. If these grow at a compound rate of 7% per year then in 10 years' time your estate will be worth £2,000,000.

However, your tax bill has increased by £400,000 a staggering near-fourfold escalation! Your tax band has jumped from 14% to 27%! There are not many people who would accept this if it was an equivalent VAT or income tax rise.

This is a mathematical trick of the trade. Governments use static allowances and inflation freezes as clever mechanisms for taking more money from their citizens without them really understanding it.

If you can understand these tricks of the trade and the mathematics involved you will enhance and preserve your wealth better than those that don't.

Starting early

We have already discussed how beneficial *time* is in generating returns to create wealth. The more time you have to achieve something, the better.

It is simple to express this mathematically using an example of two university students who start saving for retirement at different times. They both leave university at age 25 and plan to retire at 65. One starts saving from the outset while the other waits ten years. How much more do you think the one who waits 10 years has to equal the savings of his fellow student?

DOUBLE! (Assuming 7% per year returns)

Again this is a simple exposition of the power of 7% returns; because if you invest and achieve 7% per year (net of charges and tax etc.) you will double your money in 10 years. This really is worth remembering because it highlights how much more money you can accumulate if you start doing something earlier rather than later. Of course the reality is that 7% may be higher or lower than the actual returns, over this time period.

There is another way to look at this: imagine that each individual saves £10,000 over 10 years and then stops, leaving the accrued sum to increase at 7% per year thereafter, but again one starts at 25, one at 35. How much will they have at different ages?

Age	Savings achieved by early starter	Savings achieved by late starter
35	£10,000	£0
45	£20,000	£10,000
55	£40,000	£20,000
65	£80,0000	£40,000

You can see that the early starter *always* doubles his investment and by the age of 65 it is worth £40,000 more than the late starter's. The only difference (as both initially saved £10,000) is when they started!

Key Factors of the Sixth Principle:

- Compounding works mini-miracles
- Losses require disproportionate gains to get back to your starting point
- Don't pay unnecessary tax on your income or gains
- Start early!

There is no need for any individual to become a mathematical genius or worry about complex figures, but it does help to understand a few basic mathematical realities. For example, the power of compounding, the damage of big losses and how difficult they are to recover and the benefit of starting early. Support this basic understanding with a good philosophy towards financial matters and you have the necessary mind-set to create wealth.

Principle No. 7 Have a philosophy

When all is said and done money is just money.

The management of your money, your finances and financial planning are all just a means to an end; they are not an end in themselves. This is why we think having a meaningful philosophy is a powerful way to manage financial matters.

"I think therefore I am......good at handling money"

Too often mistakes are made, in money management terms, because either importance is applied to the wrong things or *too much importance* is applied to the right thing.

"The investor's chief problem - and even his worst enemy - is likely to be himself."

– Benjamin Graham

The accrual and subsequent preservation of wealth is only relevant to the benefits it provides in respect of lifestyle, peace of mind, security, family wellbeing and opportunity. If wealth is accrued for its own sake then the benefits are liable to be lost.

We discussed in our second section the value of creating a financial map. It enables you to examine how your financial future is dependent on your lifestyle choices. The map is created to provide a basis for planning your current and future financial position in line with your current and future lifestyle. This way the money side and the financial planning can equate to your lifestyle and life requirements.

This was incredibly important to Mr and Mrs Evans, the couple we used to illustrate this approach. They had very specific lifestyle requirements, dreams and ambitions. Treating these aspects as seriously as the pound and pence aspects was highly important for them.

The philosophy that we suggests works best, is the one which aims to place financial planning into its correct place within the wider life we all lead. When it requires attention it should be treated seriously and *with focus*. However, it should be seen as the means to an end; where the outcome of the financial planning is to achieve the goals set out in your financial map. This way financial planning can become enjoyable and easy, stress free and most importantly, highly effective.

The philosophy can be extended. For example, risks properly understood can help produce better returns; as an investor you can seek out areas of higher return when you understand *and accept* the risks involved.

Many people avoid risk, quite unnecessarily either because they do not understand or, more likely, are uncomfortable with it. Adjusting one's philosophy can help because the fear of risk is little more than the fear of loss. If you accept, as an investor, that losses are inevitable when you invest, then you will not be fazed or worried when they occur. You will know how to deal with them and you will know what to do.

The philosophies to avoid

We often hear crazy expressions concerning financial planning. Here are some examples:

- "I don't believe in pensions"
- "You can't go wrong with bricks and mortar"
- "Money doesn't make you happy"
- "I'll worry about my retirement when I get there"
- "My property is my pension"
- "My business will take care of me"

The issue here is one of a philosophy by default where an individual takes a financial position based on a flawed, possibly simplistic, approach which defies any logic.

Looking at some of the above examples it is easy to see why few people create wealth. However, looking at a couple of the examples in a little more detail may help us to better understand these statements.

"I don't believe in pensions" is often put forward either by people who don't save for their retirement, they choose to spend all their earnings (or more), or by those who aim to accumulate retirement savings through a building society or other investments. When someone says "I don't believe in pensions" it normally means "I don't believe the use of a pension plan is the right savings product for me to use in my financial planning". It is likely that from a financial planning perspective this is wrong; a pension plan would be a viable product to use, probably in most cases, a sensible and desirable one.

The statement will come either from ignorance or, more likely, from a perception that is based on a bad experience. "My colleague had a pension plan sold to him when he was younger and he got ripped off losing thousands of pounds" could be a typical follow up, explanatory, statement.

The "I don't believe in pensions" statement is therefore the result of some perception of pensions formed from poor (possibly third-hand) experience. Many people have poor experiences of hotels but you don't hear the statement "I don't believe in hotels" very often.

"Money doesn't make you happy" is perhaps slightly more general and based on a lifestyle view. However, even this statement belies some understanding of the nature of money and wealth creation and preservation.

It is definitely true that the pursuit of money or the reliance of money *on its own* is highly unlikely in its own right to create happiness. The link between the two things is fragile and possibly invalid. Many researchers have studied happiness in a quest to identify what the true foundation is for being happy and living a contended life. The result is that happiness is formed out of the simple things in life such as time spent with family, a job well done, experiencing nature and good health. It is not achieved through big houses, fancy cars or fast living.

Equally, good financial planning and wealth accumulation does not equate to large houses, fancy cars and fast living, but rather with creating comfort and security, peace of mind and caring for family: some of the cornerstones that make people happy.

The distinction is that money (on and of its own) is meaningless and the pursuit and love of money is a worthless quest, the pursuit and love of comfort and security is the opposite. Time and time again when asked what the most important requirement for retirement is, people answer "good health and a comfortable lifestyle". Accruing wealth will help you achieve both of these things.

The approach you have towards your financial planning will create your philosophy towards it. We suggest that the best philosophy is to remember that wealth creation is merely a means to an end. If you work towards your future goals using your financial map you will create the link between your lifestyle, life and money.

The balance between wisdom through hindsight and learning from history

There is a paradox we wish to examine which is the outcome of looking backwards!

Hindsight is a wonderful thing because in financial planning terms we can always see what the right decision would have been!

However, the serious point is that we should not spend too much time berating ourselves for mistakes once we know the outcome. Too many 'mistakes' are judged by hindsight; a poor investment or a poor decision may actually not be any such thing, because it was the right decision based on circumstances at that time.

An example of this is when people experienced poor returns from endowment policies, which were commonly used as mortgage repayment investments – especially in the 1980s and 1990s. During this period they were popular investments and few, if any, serious commentators provided warnings that they might, as proved to be the case, fail investors spectacularly. With hindsight we now know that many would have been better off choosing a repayment mortgage, but this was not considered the right choice at the time the endowment was taken out.

On the one hand we need to be philosophical and realise that financial planning is inherently a series of constantly shifting judgement calls and that inevitably the outcome is not always as required or as expected.

On the other hand history is fairly consistent and can inform us of future expectations. For example, market prices fluctuate, real assets (such as shares) tend to outperform interest based accounts and clever, new schemes or money-making ideas rarely work.

The paradox is that we have to be careful not to berate ourselves when we make mistakes but pay careful attention to the lessons from history when we make decisions about the future. Perhaps it is not a paradox at all but a simple balancing act between two parts of the same consideration!

Borrowing from other disciplines

Part of our mandate for good wealth creation and preservation is to focus on ensuring that you get the simple things right, and don't over complicate or fall foul of current trends and temptations.

In the world of health and diets just about every possible variation of a beneficial fitness regime has been put forward at one stage or another. From aerobics to Zumba, the Italian footballer's diet to the Grapefruit diet and lots more in between!

However, the basic proven ways will always succeed whereas the latest fads tend to fail. Take Pilates for example, it has a 90 year track record of delivering great results for those who follow it. Yoga, a similar discipline, has an even longer track record.

Pilates has two fundamental winning aspects, which we will describe as 'contrology' and a 'complete' body work out. Contrology is the ability to work and control the muscles with daily or weekly movements so that over time a strong, lithe, flexible body is created which is based on a strong core. The requirement for all Pilates' students is to create consistent movements that stretch the body from the core.

Secondly, it is a *complete* body work out. Although the practice focuses on the body's core, it ensures that *all* muscles are worked. The complete Pilates routine attends to the whole body ensuring that mind/body unity is developed as it works across all muscles. There is no over developed upper body with a weak lower body as seen in some muscle men.

The lessons that can be transferred from the discipline of Pilates to money management are:

1. It requires constant practice and attention

2. It requires concentration and focus

3. It is simple but highly effective

4. It exercises control

Again, it works! It is simple and effective. As with all our principles there is nothing complicated and it provides a unified approach, just as we suggest you apply to your financial planning. If you focus on your money but ignore your lifestyle, or focus on your lifestyle and ignore your money you will not achieve your potential wealth. We believe your approach to your money and wealth should be holistic: look at the whole not the individual parts.

Finally, let us look at one other parallel, this time from the world of sport.

In this case we want to study the concept of talent.

We refer you to a book called 'Bounce' by Matthew Syed, which at first glance may seem unrelated.

However, within the context of its own subject (which is mainly, but not exclusively, sport) it dismisses the concept of talent. It uses example after example, with compelling supporting evidence, to claim that talent does not exist.

Syed argues that in most cases talented sports people (this can be extended to include musicians, artists etc.) simply gained an advantage by starting early, receiving attention and coaching from an early age (giving them a step up) and along with endless hours spent practicing they were able to hone their skills and achieve champion status.

This is all based on substantial evidence which supports the view that for someone to master their discipline they will normally have spent 20,000 hours practicing.

The lesson for financial planning from this is that most success comes from constant practice and time spent within the subject area.

We suggest that anyone serious about creating wealth should:

1. Spend time and focus on their financial planning and all that goes with it – too many people simply pay too little attention to the subject

2. Find and work with experienced people who have spent hours practicing, learning and being tested on their craft and who have a proven the track record.

Key Factors of the Seventh Principle:

- Place financial planning into your life goals
- Remember money is not the be-all and end-all
- Financial Planning is a constantly shifting journey and series of judgement calls
- History and past experience is useful, but not 100% reliable, find the right balance
- Borrow from other disciplines

Just as in health matters, where the mind and body relationship is key, so it is with money matters: the balance has to be right between what you think about money and what you do about it. Money is, after all, just a means to an end. With the correct philosophy you will make better decisions and enjoy the whole process, sleeping comfortably and being stress free.

However, you are not alone! You will want and need the help of others. How to choose the right, experienced people leads us to our last principle.

Principle No. 8
Picking the right team

Picking the right team is the least obvious aspect of getting your finances right and the most important.

"Aah, but you would say that wouldn't you?" we can hear you say! Yes, it is in our interest to persuade you to choose the best team of advisers, investment managers and asset allocators, but it is extremely important.

Many amateur golfers know that when it comes to team events, four ball and foursome golf (both of which you play as a team of two), your chance of success is not dependent on how well you play in a match or series of matches, *but how successfully you choose your partner prior to a ball being struck.*

In the film 'The Godfather' based on the bestselling book by Mario Puzo there is a character called Tom Hagen (played in the film by Robert Duval). He is the adopted son of Vito Corleone (the 'Don', the head of the Mafia family). Tom Hagen is *the consigliore.*

The story is based on Puzo's intimate and researched knowledge of how Mafia's operations and how they achieved wealth and success.

"No one in his right mind would walk into the cockpit of an airplane and try to fly it, or into an operating theatre and open a belly. And yet they think nothing of managing their retirement assets. I've done all three, and I'm here to tell you that managing money is, in its most critical elements (the quota of emotional discipline and quantitative ability required) even more demanding than the first two."

– William Bernstein

Although there were infamous approaches to achieving this, nothing was more important to the family than the consigliore. His role was key. He was the adviser to the Don: the person who made everything run smoothly, who ensured that all angles were covered in deals and with personnel. He was entrusted to keep everything together and protect all the component parts of the empire.

Anyone with wealth – at whatever stage - should have a consigliore or the modern financial services equivalent; someone who is an adviser, fixer, trusted source of support and help.

This financial 'consigliore' can ensure that everything is right for their client; they can provide the glue which binds together every part of the financial map and wealth requirement.

The team

How do you pick your team?

Here is the good news. You are blessed when it comes to choosing and appointing your wealth management team. You are unbounded by the restrictions that apply in so many other areas.

If you want a doctor or a dentist you are probably tied to your local town or district; if you want a lawyer you will probably have to pay much more for the best than for a second rate lawyer. But in financial affairs there are no geographical restrictions and the best practitioners probably **cost no more than the average or the worst**.

We have aimed to demonstrate in early sections that the accumulation and preservation of wealth is mainly about simple steps and actions performed very well. In addition small differences in approach and getting minor details *just right* can lead to major differences in eventual, long term outcomes.

In this respect your team is key. Helping you to establish the details and arranging, at every level and in every respect, for the right structure to be in place. Before we answer the question of how to pick your team, we should first look at the team you will need to put in place.

This may include:

- An adviser or planner who can help with your strategy and put together a personal plan of action (your 'map')

- One or more people to help with the allocation of your invested money

- An accountant to help with your tax affairs including tax returns

- Companies or people to manage the holding areas for your accumulating wealth. Fund managers, for example

Alternatively, you could do it all yourself.

The DIY approach

There are many people who do not trust the financial industry, believing that advisers, stockbrokers, money managers and fund managers are either in it for their own benefit or are not up to the job (or arguably both). These individuals believe they are better off doing their own financial planning, investing and tax planning.

This is, of course, an absolute right of any individual to take this view and stance. After all, it is their life and their money.

Not trusting the financial industry is understandable after the scandals of the past, especially given the financial crisis of 2008, which exposed great swathes of the financial industry to be seriously out of control. It is not helped by the likes of Bernie Madoff in America running a massive Ponzi scheme, literally robbing wealthy people of hundreds of millions of dollars.

Scandals and the infamous cases are the exception rather than the rule, although bad practice is found in many industries. Naturally, bad news stories dominate the news coverage and receive a great deal publicity, for example when a doctor starts poisoning his patients it is going to make the headlines.

Every industry has problems and bad apples.

If you have a poor meal in a restaurant do you stop going to restaurants? It is more likely you will not go to that particular restaurant again, but you will still go to other restaurants.

The only reason therefore to reject using specialist help is if you either perceive there is a systemic problem within a part of the industry, or you think you can do better yourself.

Here are some of the pitfalls of the DIY approach which may not be immediately obvious:

- Using specialists in different areas may offer you regulatory protections (including access to compensation schemes) which you would not get through DIY

- Specialists may have access to information which is not available to you

- They may have knowledge of programs and facilities you can access which are either expensive for you to obtain DIY or which are simply not available

- They may have access to investments which cannot be accessed directly

- They should, hopefully, have wide expertise and good experience

- They will have the time and resources to dedicate to the often time consuming areas of financial planning

The DIY option is viable, but if you can find a good team you will provide yourself with a much greater chance of achieving all of the result that you desire.

The problem with experts

"Can I borrow your watch to tell you the time?" The difficulty we have as buyers of a commodity or service is knowing what to look for. Anyone can call themselves - or claim to be - an expert (and many do!). But what is an expert – how do you find one and what difference does it make?

Expertise is a combination of *knowledge* and *skill*. It is this blend that defines the expert. Many people have skills and many people have knowledge; what we want is someone who has the right balance between the two and a proven basis for delivering this.

Fortunately, the modern financial world is one where standards have risen and regulation has tightened. This has created greater transparency – you can now ask to see someone's qualifications. This has not always been the case. In many ways the financial services market was – for decades - a 'wild west'; just about anyone could set up and provide a service (e.g. financial advice). Or the benchmarks for entering the 'industry' were so low, it allowed entrepreneurial spirits to pass a few quick exams and appoint themselves as experts overnight. Many people have happily entrusted their financial affairs to such low grade specialists.

This would be like get into a 400 seater passenger jet flown by a pilot who had taken a few lessons at his local flying school.

Self-appointed experts are a danger to anyone serious about creating or protecting wealth. The value of a true expert is enormous. It is so enormous that it is worth taking time over and, arguably, is likely to be the biggest single differentiator in how well you manage your position.

Too few people seeking to prosper financially go about this step in the right way.

Picking a financial planner

As we stated earlier the consigliore was critical to the Mafia family and business. You can have the best enforcers but if you have a weak consigliore you will have big problems and so it is with financial planning. The key is to choose the best financial planner possible and everything else will look after itself.

Your financial planner will help you develop your financial map and build the asset allocation process to support it (including whether you should invest passively or actively, directly or indirectly and what vehicles to use). Together you can review your arrangements regularly to ensure that, over time, everything is managed successfully.

They become your consigliore, helping with the big picture and the day to day issues.

Although we have outlined that the basic principles of wealth success have remained unchanged, the financial world does constantly change and will continue to do so. Your financial planner will help you understand and assess these changes: they will provide information, updates and a view on how they may impact you on a regular basis.

Your financial planner is extremely valuable when problems occur, helping to facilitate the correction of any errors. They can also relieve some of the paperwork, correspondence and forms. Overall, their role is twofold, to assist with the strategic approach ('the big picture') and with the daily tasks. **Selecting your financial planner is too important to leave to chance.**

What to look for when you decide to use a financial planner:

- Experience

- Qualifications – do they have the best qualifications available? Less than 1 in 10 financial planners have achieved Chartered status, an important demonstration of quality

- A clear and easy to follow process

- Evidence from others who have had a valuable and beneficial experience with that financial planner

- A happy and successful team within that firm

In chapter two, we met Mr and Mrs Evans, who were at a crucial stage of their lives, looking to get clarity around their positions and reach some decisions about how and when to strike out into retirement.

Their biggest and, arguably, most important decision was not what tax structures to use or which pension funds to place their money into, or anything of this sort; their big decision was who to use to help them best navigate the waters in front of them.

That was their biggest challenge, to find someone who could provide exceptional help and support. The difference between getting that decision right or wrong could easily account for more financial gain or loss than any other single decision.

We like to think Mr and Mrs Evans got their decision spot on!

Picking your team

It is surprising that even when there is no structural approach in place, or when individuals decide to work on their own (adopting a DIY approach), there ends up being a team in place. In such instances it is a team by default: which has not been selected according to any meaningful screening or criteria.

Many people have accountants they have found in a directory, fund managers they have chosen based on past performance league tables (even though sometimes the actual fund manager may not have been responsible for the past performance) and others who have been selected for relatively random reasons. A stockbroker who is a friend of a friend, for example.

We have already considered the criteria for choosing your financial planner and this same criteria also applies to choosing your team. Remember that your financial planner can also advise on the selection of your team. Find experienced firms and individuals with a proven track record. The old adage applies here "there are no old and bold pilots"; you cannot beat the tried and tested.

The team needs people to help with the asset allocation, fund management and investment selection. With regard to fund management your biggest decisions will be directed by your asset allocation requirements. From these you should seek out the best, most reliable and consistent funds (assuming funds are your chosen route and you want an element of active approach). You should also ensure the selection is based on past performance, but with a filter applied for consistency, managed risk and reasonable costs.

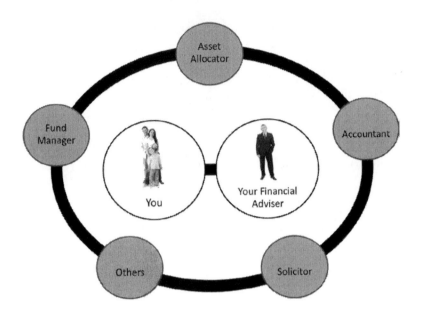

In an earlier section we used the analogy of working your personal finances in a way that is akin to a good business and we think it is beneficial to end on the same note. Good businesses are built on strong foundations which will always embody certain standards:

- A well-structured and well executed business plan

- Sound financial management

- Working with the best people in the business

The business of personal financial management has the same basic requirements. Get your team right, especially your 'consigliore' and you will put the final part of your overall financial plan in place. A financial plan which will ensure you create and protect wealth for you and your family.

Key Factors of the Eighth Principle:

- Picking your team and working with the best people is probably the single, most important, financial decision you will ever take
- Test and check the expertise of those you work with

You will need a team to help get your financial plans in place and thereafter to manage those plans throughout the years. Picking this team could end up being your most important decision. Find and work with the best and you will not go far wrong.

Conclusion

It is strange that two of the most important elements in many people's lives, parenting and managing money are largely ignored within the educational system. More effort is put into teaching French than teaching young people how to be a good parent or how to manage money.

Unfortunately there is a break down here, most people become good parents through genetic instinct, love and common sense. The same does not apply to managing money.

The money business is a supply and demand business. The suppliers, for example banks, investment companies and credit card providers are often handsomely rewarded for encouraging bad habits or bad practice amongst the consumer - the demand side. In this respect the financial industry can be compared with, and is as controversial as, the tobacco companies. There is often a clash between what is good for the goose and what is good for the gander!

There is only one way this will ever change.

The consumer has to know what is best for them. This can only happen through foundational education. If every person is taught the sound principles of financial planning then the status quo can change.

Our reason for writing this book is simple: we wish to help provide such foundational education. We consider it is part of our role to help people understand financial planning and its importance to their future wellbeing.

As an individual reading this book you can change your life by acquiring such an education. You do not need to know every aspect of financial planning, but you do need to know the fundamental elements which are described here as the eight key principles.

As with so many things, what is good for the individual is good for society. If enough people achieve foundational experience and understanding it will start to make a difference across the whole economy. This may appear to be a sweeping statement but more profitable investments will result in improved economic activity and create jobs. There will be less reliance on the State and as a consequence the State can help those who are worse off and in need of help. There population will be wealthier: and it is a truism that the wealthier you are, the more likely you are to be healthy and live longer. The outcomes from a general improvement in financial education could be dramatic.

Only you can make the necessary changes required to impact *you*. We hope therefore that this book has provided you with the incentive to be more financially prepared and – dare we hope this as well – that you come to enjoy the process of financial planning.

The benefit for you is that if you do achieve these two ideals you will create wealth for yourself and your family and, thereafter, you will preserve and protect it.

That is the wealth secret in a nutshell – become really good at financial planning and everything else will take care of itself.

Penguin

About Penguin Wealth

Penguin is a Financial Planning firm in Cardiff, formed in 2010 by a group of Financial Planners with a shared vision and a love for their jobs.

"Our purpose is to make a positive difference by exceeding expectations, one relationship at a time"

The Penguin Advice team believe they have the best jobs in the world! They get to help you plan for a more comfortable and enjoyable future. How could we not find satisfaction in that?

Penguin's founders share a vision of continuous professional development. It is their mission to become the best they can possibly be, to continuously learn and progress so that they can stay on top of the latest industry developments and provide their clients, and the community, with the best possible advice.

Penguin are now reaping the rewards of this development and growth, winning several major awards over the last few years, including 'Adviser firm of the year Wales' at the Professional Adviser Awards.

Penguin were also the first firm in the UK to become IFP Accredited, CII Chartered and BS8577 Certified. Signifying that we "demonstrate the highest professional standards of financial planning service and advice", "our clients are at the heart of our business" and that we "ensure our staff members acquire and retain the necessary knowledge and skills to deliver the highest quality advice".

Penguin is a trading name of Penguin Wealth LLP who are authorised and regulated by the Financial Conduct Authority. FCA No. 581108

About The Author

Craig is a Certified Financial Planner, Chartered Wealth Manager and a board member of the Institute of Financial Planning.

Craig started in Financial Services in 2000 and considers himself extremely fortunate that he's found his vocation.

Hard work and constant study has resulted in Craig reaching Certified Financial Planner, a level of qualification that only the top 1% reach. Craig was recently voted as the top IFA in Cardiff by VouchedFor.co.uk – a website where clients can review their financial adviser.

Craig really enjoys presenting at seminars as he is passionate about sharing his knowledge with people who need it. This is evidenced further by Craig authoring a book that will be featured on Amazon upon its release.

On a personal note, Craig has always lived in Cardiff and considers himself lucky to be blessed with 2 children and 3 step children. He loves playing and reading with his little ones and sharing as much time as he can with his family.

Contributions to this book were also made by Gavin Baos, Mike Carberry and Oliver Pughe of Penguin Wealth's Advice Team.

For more information on Penguin Wealth please visit our website at: www.penguinwealth.com

Tel: 02920 450143
Fax: 02920 450641
Email: info@penguinwealth.com